First World War
and Army of Occupation
War Diary
France, Belgium and Germany

30 DIVISION
89 Infantry Brigade
King's (Liverpool Regiment)
19th Battalion
6 November 1915 - 30 June 1918

WO95/2334/2

The Naval & Military Press Ltd
www.nmarchive.com
Published in association with The National Archives

Published by

The Naval & Military Press Ltd

Unit 10 Ridgewood Industrial Park,

Uckfield, East Sussex,

TN22 5QE England

Tel: +44 (0) 1825 749494

www.naval-military-press.com

www.nmarchive.com

This diary has been reprinted in facsimile from the original. Any imperfections are inevitably reproduced and the quality may fall short of modern type and cartographic standards.

© Crown Copyright
Images reproduced by permission of The National Archives, London, England, 2015.

Contents

Document type	Place/Title	Date From	Date To
Heading	17th Kings Liverpool Nov 15-June 18		
Heading	30th Division 89th Infy Bde 17th Bn King's L'Pools Nov 1915-jun 1918 To U K		
Heading	30th Division 17th Liverpools Vol I Nov 15 June 1918		
War Diary	Lark Hill Camp Salisbury Plain	06/11/1915	06/11/1915
War Diary	Ostrehove Camp Boulogne	07/11/1915	07/11/1915
War Diary	Bellancourt	09/11/1915	16/11/1915
War Diary	Sur Camps	17/11/1915	17/11/1915
War Diary	Vignacourt	18/11/1915	27/11/1915
War Diary	Beaumetz Somme	28/11/1915	30/11/1915
Heading	30th Div 17th L'Pool Rgt. Vol 2		
Heading	Confidential War Diary Of 17th (Service) Batt The Liverpool From 1.12.15 To 31.12.15 (Volume II December 1915)		
War Diary	Beaumetz Somme	01/12/1915	15/12/1915
War Diary	Beaumetz	16/12/1915	16/12/1915
War Diary	Puchevillers	16/12/1915	16/12/1915
War Diary	Engle Belmer	20/12/1915	20/12/1915
War Diary	Mesnil	20/12/1915	20/12/1915
War Diary	Hamel	20/12/1915	20/12/1915
War Diary	Auchonvillers	21/12/1915	21/12/1915
War Diary	Englebelmer	21/12/1915	21/12/1915
War Diary	Hamel	21/12/1915	21/12/1915
War Diary	Mesnil	01/12/1915	21/12/1915
War Diary	Englebelmer	22/12/1915	22/12/1915
War Diary	Mesnil	22/12/1915	23/12/1915
War Diary	Auchonvillers	24/12/1915	24/12/1915
War Diary	Hamel	24/12/1915	24/12/1915
War Diary	Engle Belmer	25/12/1915	25/12/1915
War Diary	Puchvillers	25/12/1915	26/12/1915
War Diary	Beaumetz	26/12/1915	31/12/1915
Heading	30th Div. 17th L'Pool Vol. 3 Tam 16		
War Diary	Naours	05/01/1916	05/01/1916
War Diary	Pont Noyelles	05/01/1916	06/01/1916
War Diary	Sailly Lorette	06/01/1916	07/01/1916
War Diary	Suzanne	07/01/1916	08/01/1916
War Diary	Maricourt Sector A 4	08/01/1916	10/01/1916
War Diary	Defences	10/01/1916	12/01/1916
War Diary	Mari Court Sector A 4	12/01/1916	16/01/1916
War Diary	Suzanne	17/01/1916	20/01/1916
War Diary	Maricourt A 4	20/01/1916	21/01/1916
War Diary	Mari Court Sector A 4	21/01/1916	24/01/1916
War Diary	Mari Court Defences	24/01/1916	31/01/1916
Heading	Confidential War Diary Of 17th Bn Liverpool Regt Volume IV From 1-2-16 To 29-2-16		
War Diary	Mari Court Defences	01/02/1916	02/02/1916
War Diary	Sub Sector A4 Maricourt	02/02/1916	06/02/1916
War Diary	Mari Court Defences	06/02/1916	07/02/1916
War Diary	Suzanne	08/02/1916	10/02/1916
War Diary	A 4	11/02/1916	13/02/1916

War Diary	A 4 Sub Sector	12/02/1916	16/02/1916
War Diary	Bray	17/02/1916	18/02/1916
War Diary	Daours	18/02/1916	26/02/1916
War Diary	Corbie	26/02/1916	26/02/1916
War Diary	Etinehem	26/02/1916	28/02/1916
War Diary	A1 Sub Sector Mari Court	28/02/1916	29/02/1916
Heading	17th Liverpools Vol 5		
War Diary	A 1 Mari Court	01/03/1916	01/03/1916
War Diary	Z 1 Mari Court	02/03/1916	03/03/1916
War Diary	Etinehem	03/03/1916	05/03/1916
War Diary	Z 1	06/03/1916	08/03/1916
War Diary	Mari Court Defences	09/03/1916	12/03/1916
War Diary	Z 1	12/03/1916	16/03/1916
War Diary	Grovetown Camp	17/03/1916	17/03/1916
War Diary	Corbie	17/03/1916	18/03/1916
War Diary	Franvillers	18/03/1916	28/03/1916
War Diary	Etinehem Camp	29/03/1916	31/03/1916
Heading	Confidential War Diary Of 7th Battalion Kings Liverpool Regiment. From 1st April 1916 To 30th April 1916 (Volume 6)		
War Diary	Etinehem Camp	01/04/1916	30/04/1916
War Diary	Z 1	30/04/1916	30/04/1916
Heading	Confidential War Diary 17th (Ser) Div. The King's (Liverpool Regt). From 1.5.1916 To 31.5.1916 Volume VII		
War Diary	Z 1	01/05/1916	05/05/1916
War Diary	Maricourt Defences	06/05/1916	11/05/1916
War Diary	Z 1	11/05/1916	17/05/1916
War Diary	Etinehem	18/05/1916	24/05/1916
War Diary	Vaux-En-Amienois	25/05/1916	26/05/1916
Heading	17th King's L Pool June 1916		
War Diary	Vaux-En-Amienois	10/06/1916	12/06/1916
War Diary	Heilly	12/06/1916	12/06/1916
War Diary	Bray	15/06/1916	17/06/1916
War Diary	Mari Court Defences	18/06/1916	30/06/1916
Heading	War Diary Of 17th Bn. King's (Liverpool) Regt For July 1916		
Heading	Confidential War Diary Of 17th Bn. King's (Liverpool) Regiment From 1st July 1916 To 31st July 1916 Volume 9		
War Diary	Z 2 Sub Sector	01/07/1916	01/07/1916
War Diary	Dublin Trench	03/07/1916	05/07/1916
War Diary	Bois de Tailles	06/07/1916	08/07/1916
War Diary	Trigger Wood	09/07/1916	09/07/1916
War Diary	Trones Wood	10/07/1916	13/07/1916
War Diary	Trigger Wood	13/07/1916	13/07/1916
War Diary	Bois Des Tailles	14/07/1916	14/07/1916
War Diary	Corbie	14/07/1916	19/07/1916
War Diary	Happy Valley	20/07/1916	20/07/1916
War Diary	PT 7 1 North	21/07/1916	31/07/1916
Diagram etc	Notes by Lt. Colonel B.C. Fairfax Commanding 17th Bn. The King's on the fighting at Trones wood 10th, 11th & 12th July 1916	15/07/1916	15/07/1916
Heading	89th Brigade 30th Division 1/17th Battalion The King's Liverpool Regiment August 1916		
War Diary	Citadel Camp Pt 71 North	01/08/1916	02/08/1916

War Diary	Dernancourt	02/08/1916	02/08/1916
War Diary	Longpres	02/08/1916	02/08/1916
War Diary	Doudelainville	02/08/1916	03/08/1916
War Diary	Pont Remy	03/08/1916	03/08/1916
War Diary	Merville	04/08/1916	04/08/1916
War Diary	Calonne	04/08/1916	10/08/1916
War Diary	Les La Bes	10/08/1916	18/08/1916
War Diary	Hingette	18/08/1916	23/08/1916
War Diary	La Pannerie	24/08/1916	25/08/1916
War Diary	Hingette	26/08/1916	27/08/1916
War Diary	Gorre	27/08/1916	31/08/1916
War Diary	Givenchy Sector	31/08/1916	31/08/1916
Heading	Confidential War Diary. Of 17th Bn. King's Liverpool Regt. From 1st September 1916 To 30th September 1916 (Volume XI)		
War Diary	Givenchy Left Sub Sector	01/09/1916	05/09/1916
War Diary	Village Line	06/09/1916	08/09/1916
War Diary	Bethune	08/09/1916	14/09/1916
War Diary	Savy	14/09/1916	14/09/1916
War Diary	Ecoivres	14/09/1916	17/09/1916
War Diary	Villers Chatel	17/09/1916	19/09/1916
War Diary	Gezain Court	20/09/1916	21/09/1916
War Diary	Vignacourt	22/09/1916	04/10/1916
War Diary	Dernancourt	05/10/1916	11/10/1916
War Diary	Gird Trench And Gird Support	11/10/1916	13/10/1916
War Diary	S. 26. Central	13/10/1916	20/10/1916
War Diary	Crest Trench	21/10/1916	22/10/1916
War Diary	Mametz Wood Camp	22/10/1916	24/10/1916
War Diary	Buire Sous Corbie	24/10/1916	26/10/1916
War Diary	Halloy	27/10/1916	28/10/1916
War Diary	Pommier	28/10/1916	31/10/1916
Heading	Confidential War Diary Of 17th Battn Kings (Liverpool) Regiment. From 1st November 1916 To 30th November 1916 Volume 13		
War Diary		01/11/1916	04/11/1916
War Diary	Bienvillers	04/11/1916	16/11/1916
War Diary	Pommier	16/11/1916	18/11/1916
War Diary	Humbercamps	18/11/1916	28/11/1916
War Diary	Berles	29/11/1916	30/11/1916
Heading	Confidential War Diary Of 17th Battalion Kings Liverpool Regiment From 1st December 1916 To 31st December 1916 Volume 14		
War Diary	Berles	01/12/1916	10/12/1916
War Diary	Humber Camps	10/12/1916	17/12/1916
War Diary	Reference Map. Ransart 51.c. S.E. 3 & 4 (Parts of) Edition 3.c. 1/10000	17/12/1916	22/12/1916
War Diary	Berles	22/12/1916	31/12/1916
War Diary	Humber Camps	01/01/1917	08/01/1917
War Diary	Halloy	08/01/1917	31/01/1917
Heading	Confidential War Diary. of 17th Battalion Kings Liverpool Regiment. From 1st February 1917 To 28th February 1917		
War Diary	Halloy	01/02/1917	05/02/1917
War Diary	Simen Court	05/02/1917	06/02/1917
War Diary	Arras	06/02/1917	28/02/1917

Heading	Confidential War Diary Of 17th Battalion King's Liverpool Regiment From 1st March 1917 To 31st March 1917 Volume 17		
Heading	Minor Operations.		
War Diary	Arras	01/03/1917	22/03/1917
War Diary	Agny	23/03/1917	23/03/1917
War Diary	Bretencourt	24/03/1917	24/03/1917
War Diary	Basseux	25/03/1917	25/03/1917
War Diary	Saulty	26/03/1917	31/03/1917
War Diary	Third Army.	09/03/1917	09/03/1917
Miscellaneous	VIIth. Corps. G.847. 8th. March. 1917	08/03/1917	08/03/1917
Miscellaneous	89th Brigade No. B. 156. Head Quarters 30th Division.	08/03/1917	08/03/1917
Miscellaneous	Report On German Raid.	08/03/1917	08/03/1917
Map	Map. Neuville Vitasse M. 14.c.	08/03/1917	08/03/1917
Miscellaneous	C Form (Original). Messages And Signals.		
Heading	Confidential. War Diary. of 17th Battalion King's Liverpool Regiment. From 1st April 1917 to 30th April 1917. Volume No. 18		
War Diary	Saulty	01/04/1917	01/04/1917
War Diary	Bavincourt	02/04/1917	03/04/1917
War Diary	Blairville & Ficheux	04/04/1917	08/04/1917
War Diary	Sun Kim Road N of Boisleux	09/04/1917	09/04/1917
War Diary	Nagpur Trench	10/04/1917	11/04/1917
War Diary	N Of Henin	11/04/1917	12/04/1917
War Diary	Blairville	13/04/1917	14/04/1917
War Diary	Couin	14/04/1917	20/04/1917
War Diary	Beau Rains	20/04/1917	23/04/1917
War Diary	Neuville Vitasse	23/04/1917	23/04/1917
War Diary	E of Heninel	24/04/1917	24/04/1917
War Diary	N 29 a 1/3	25/04/1917	25/04/1917
War Diary	N 30 B.	25/04/1917	28/04/1917
War Diary	Hindenburg System	29/04/1917	29/04/1917
War Diary	Haute-Cote	29/04/1917	30/04/1917
Operation(al) Order(s)	Operation Order No. 56 By Lieut. Col. J.N. Peck. N.C. Commanding 17th Battn. King's Liverpool Regt.	07/04/1917	07/04/1917
Operation(al) Order(s)	Amendment To Operation Order No. 56	07/04/1917	07/04/1917
Operation(al) Order(s)	Supplement To Operation Order No. 56.-17th K.L.R. Action Of Machine Guns.	07/04/1917	07/04/1917
Heading	Confidential. War Diary. of 17th Bn. The King's (Liverpool Regiment). From 1st May 1917. To). 1st May 1917. (Volume 19)		
War Diary	Haute Cote	01/05/1917	03/05/1917
War Diary	Fortel	03/05/1917	14/05/1917
War Diary	Bachimont	15/05/1917	16/05/1917
War Diary	Bachimont Le Poncnel Vaulx	17/05/1917	20/05/1917
War Diary	Haute Cote	20/05/1917	21/05/1917
War Diary	Valhuon	21/05/1917	22/05/1917
War Diary	St. Hilaire	22/05/1917	24/05/1917
War Diary	Steen Becque (Le Bas)	24/05/1917	25/05/1917
War Diary	Caestre	25/05/1917	26/05/1917
War Diary	Steen Voorde	26/05/1917	28/05/1917
War Diary	Brandhoek	28/05/1917	29/05/1917
War Diary	Support Trenches	30/05/1917	31/05/1917
Heading	Confidential. War Diary. of 17th Bn The Kings (Liverpool Regiment). From June 1st 1917 To June 30th 1917. (Volume 20)		

War Diary	Support Trenches	01/06/1917	05/06/1917
War Diary	Ypres	05/06/1917	06/06/1917
War Diary	Support Trenches	06/06/1917	08/06/1917
War Diary	Poperinghe Abeele Area	09/06/1917	20/06/1917
War Diary	Canal Reserve Camp. (Dickebusch)	21/06/1917	24/06/1917
War Diary	Canal Reserve Camp.	25/06/1917	27/06/1917
War Diary	Chateau Segard	28/06/1917	28/06/1917
War Diary	Front Line Trenches.	29/06/1917	30/06/1917
Heading	Confidential. War 1Diary. of 17th Battalion The King's Liverpool Regiment. From 1st July 1917 To 31st July 1917 Volume 21		
War Diary	Front Line Trenches.	01/07/1917	07/07/1917
War Diary	Ottawa Camp	07/07/1917	07/07/1917
War Diary	Busseboom	07/07/1917	07/07/1917
War Diary	Watten	07/07/1917	07/07/1917
War Diary	Blanc Pignon	07/07/1917	19/07/1917
War Diary	Le Temple (Near Steenvoorde)	19/07/1917	24/07/1917
War Diary	Connaught Camp	24/07/1917	28/07/1917
War Diary	Palace Camp	28/07/1917	29/07/1917
War Diary	Chateau Segard	30/07/1917	30/07/1917
War Diary	Promenade Trench	31/07/1917	31/07/1917
Heading	Confidential. War Diary. of 17th Bn The King's Liverpool Regt. From 1st August 1917 To 31st August 1917 (Volume 22)		
War Diary		01/08/1917	03/08/1917
War Diary	Chateau Segard	04/08/1917	04/08/1917
War Diary	Ottawa Camp	05/08/1917	05/08/1917
War Diary	Godewaersvelde	05/08/1917	07/08/1917
War Diary	Outter Steene	07/08/1917	10/08/1917
War Diary	Camp Near St. Jans Cappel	10/08/1917	23/08/1917
War Diary	Dranoutre	23/08/1917	29/08/1917
War Diary	Camp At N. 25. B. 8/2	29/08/1917	31/08/1917
Heading	Confidential. War Diary. of 17th Bn the King's Liverpool Regt. From 1-9-1917 To 30-9-1917 (Volume XXIII)		
War Diary	Camp At N.28.b. 8/2	01/09/1917	02/09/1917
War Diary	Supports (Right Battalion Hollebeke Sector)	02/09/1917	09/09/1917
War Diary	Front Line. Hollebeke Sector	09/09/1917	17/09/1917
War Diary	Front Line	18/09/1917	19/09/1917
War Diary	Support Area	20/09/1917	20/09/1917
War Diary	Parrain Farm	20/09/1917	30/09/1917
Heading	Confidential. War Diary. of 17th Battalion The King's (Liverpool Regiment.) From 1st October 1917 To 31st October 1917 Volume 24		
War Diary	Parrain Farm Camp	01/10/1917	11/10/1917
War Diary	Support Area Hollebeke Sector	11/10/1917	16/10/1917
War Diary	Front Line. Hollebeke Sector	16/10/1917	21/10/1917
War Diary	Parrain Farm Camp	22/10/1917	29/10/1917
War Diary	Ramillies Camp	29/10/1917	31/10/1917
War Diary	Support Area Hollebeke Sector	31/10/1917	31/10/1917
Heading	Confidential War Diary of 17th Bn. The King's (Liverpool Regt) From 1st November 1917 To 30th November 1917 (Volume 25)		
War Diary	Support Area	01/11/1917	01/11/1917
War Diary	Hollebeke Sector	02/11/1917	05/11/1917
War Diary	Front Line	06/11/1917	06/11/1917

War Diary	Hollebeke Sector	07/11/1917	10/11/1917
War Diary	Front Line	10/11/1917	10/11/1917
War Diary	Hollebeke Sector	11/11/1917	11/11/1917
War Diary	Ramillies Camp	11/11/1917	13/11/1917
War Diary	Wakefield Huts	13/11/1917	15/11/1917
War Diary	Locre	16/11/1917	16/11/1917
War Diary	Steen Voorde	16/11/1917	27/11/1917
War Diary	Chippewa Camp	27/11/1917	30/11/1917
Heading	Confidential War Diary 17th Bn. The King's (Liverpool Regiment) From 1st December 1917 To 31st December 1917 Volume 26		
War Diary	Chippawa Camp	01/12/1917	03/12/1917
War Diary	Front Line Polderhoek Sector	04/12/1917	07/12/1917
War Diary	Torr Top Tunnel	08/12/1917	12/12/1917
War Diary	Scottish Wood Camp	13/12/1917	14/12/1917
War Diary	Torr Top Tunnel	15/12/1917	16/12/1917
War Diary	Scottish Wood Camp	17/12/1917	18/12/1917
War Diary	Front Line Polderhoek Sector	19/12/1917	21/12/1917
War Diary	Support Sector Stirling Castle	22/12/1917	24/12/1917
War Diary	Chippawa Camp	25/12/1917	30/12/1917
War Diary	Front Line Polderhoek Sector	31/12/1917	31/12/1917
Heading	Confidential War Diary Of 17th (Service) Battn. The King's (Liverpool Regt). From 1st January 1918 To 31st January 1918 (Volume 27)		
War Diary	Front Line Polderhoek Sector	01/01/1918	02/01/1918
War Diary	Torr Top Tunnel	03/01/1918	06/01/1918
War Diary	Shan Chateau	06/01/1918	07/01/1918
War Diary	Campagne	07/01/1918	11/01/1918
War Diary	Fouencamps	12/01/1918	13/01/1918
War Diary	Marcelcave	13/01/1918	14/01/1918
War Diary	Harbonnieres	14/01/1918	18/01/1918
War Diary	Davenscourt	18/01/1918	19/01/1918
War Diary	Champien	19/01/1918	26/01/1918
War Diary	Libermont	26/01/1918	27/01/1918
War Diary	Marest	27/01/1918	28/01/1918
War Diary	Viry-Noureuil	28/01/1918	29/01/1918
War Diary	Front Line	29/01/1918	31/01/1918
Heading	Confidential. War Diary of 17th Bn. The King's (Liverpool Regt) From 1st February 1918. To 28th February (Volume 28)		
War Diary	St. Firmin-Travecy Sector	01/02/1918	03/02/1918
War Diary	Fargnier	03/02/1918	08/02/1918
War Diary	Caillouel	09/02/1918	09/02/1918
War Diary	Muirancourt	09/02/1918	10/02/1918
War Diary	Avricourt.	10/02/1918	20/02/1918
War Diary	Flavy-Le-Meldeux	20/02/1918	21/02/1918
War Diary	Aubigny	21/02/1918	22/02/1918
War Diary	Fluquieres	22/02/1918	28/02/1918
Heading	89th Inf. Bde. 30th Div. War Diary 17th Battn. The King's (Liverpool Regiment). March 1918		
Heading	Confidential. War Diary 17th Battalion The King's (Liverpool Regiment) From March 1st 1918 To March 31st 1918 Volume No 29		
War Diary	St. Quentin Right Sub. Sector	01/03/1918	09/03/1918
War Diary	Vaux	10/03/1918	18/03/1918
War Diary	Villers St. Christophe	18/03/1918	21/03/1918

War Diary	Beauvois	21/03/1918	21/03/1918
War Diary	Atilly	21/03/1918	22/03/1918
War Diary	Aviation Wood	22/03/1918	22/03/1918
War Diary	Ham	22/03/1919	23/03/1919
War Diary	Verlaines	23/03/1918	24/03/1918
War Diary	Esmery Hallon	24/03/1918	24/03/1918
War Diary	Moyen Court	24/03/1918	25/03/1918
War Diary	Roiglise	25/03/1918	25/03/1918
War Diary	Plessier	26/03/1918	26/03/1918
War Diary	Folies	26/03/1918	28/03/1918
War Diary	Mezieres	28/03/1918	28/03/1918
War Diary	Rouvrel	28/03/1918	30/03/1918
War Diary	St. Valery Sur. Somme	31/03/1918	31/03/1918
War Diary	Nibas	31/03/1918	31/03/1918
Heading	Confidential War Diary Of 17th Battalion The King's (Liverpool Regiment) From 1st April 1918 To 30th April 1918 Volume XXX		
War Diary	Nibas St. Valery-Sur-Ref Map:- Abbeville Sheet-14 1.100.000	01/04/1918	04/04/1918
War Diary	Bridge Camp No. 1 Elverdinghe B.14.d. Sheet 28. 1.40.000	05/04/1918	07/04/1918
War Diary	Poelcappelle-Sector-Support Line	07/04/1918	10/04/1918
War Diary	Poelcappelle Sector. Front Line System	11/04/1918	12/04/1918
War Diary	Poelcappelle-Sector-Forward Support Zones	13/04/1918	16/04/1918
War Diary	Lennox Camp (B.17.c.5.3) Sheet 28 N.E. 1.20.000	17/04/1918	17/04/1918
War Diary	Westoutre-Mont-Kokereel Road (M.8.d) Sheet 28 SE. 1.20.000	18/04/1918	18/04/1918
War Diary	Front Line South East St Jans Cappel Sheet 28. S. IV. 1.20.000	19/04/1918	19/04/1918
War Diary	R.11.b. Sheet 27 SE 1.20.000	20/04/1918	21/04/1918
War Diary	Busseboom Scottish Camp Dominion Camp (G.22.b) Sheet 28 NW. 1.20.000	21/04/1918	23/04/1918
War Diary	Scottish & Dominion Camps Busseboom	23/04/1918	25/04/1918
War Diary	Voormezeele Sector	25/04/1918	29/04/1918
War Diary	Voormezeele Defence	29/04/1918	30/04/1918
Heading	Confidential War Diary Of 17th Battalion "The King's" (L'pool Regt) For The Month Of May-1918-1st To 31st May. 1918 Volume XXXI		
War Diary	Voormezeele Defences	01/05/1918	01/05/1918
War Diary	Scottish Camp	02/05/1918	02/05/1918
War Diary	St. Lawrence Camp	02/05/1918	05/05/1918
War Diary	Vierstraat Sector-In Bde. Reserve	06/05/1918	08/05/1918
War Diary	Vierstraat Sector	08/05/1918	10/05/1918
War Diary	St. Lawrence Camp	11/05/1918	11/05/1918
War Diary	Buysscheure	11/05/1918	15/05/1918
War Diary	Woincourt	16/05/1918	16/05/1918
War Diary	Meneslies	17/05/1918	26/05/1918
War Diary	Incheville	26/05/1918	31/05/1918
Heading	Confidential War Diary Of 17th Battalion "The King's" (Liverpool Regiment.) For The Month Of June 1918 1st 30th June 1918 Volume XXXII		
War Diary	Incheville	01/06/1918	21/06/1918
War Diary	Vismes-Au-Val	21/06/1918	22/06/1918
War Diary	Ailly-Le-Haut Clocher	22/06/1918	28/06/1918
War Diary	St. Riquier Abbeville	28/06/1918	29/06/1918
War Diary	Boulogne	29/06/1918	30/06/1918

War Diary	Folkestone	30/06/1918	30/06/1918
War Diary	Aldershot	30/06/1918	30/06/1918
War Diary	Mytchett Camp	30/06/1918	30/06/1918
War Diary	Movement Order By Lieut. Col. J.P. Pitts. M.C. Comdg. 17th Bn. The King's (Liverpool Regt.)		
Miscellaneous	Movement Order By Lieut. Col. J.P. Pitts. M.C. Comdg. 17th Bn. The King's (Liverpool Regt.)	27/06/1918	27/06/1918
Miscellaneous	17th King's Liverpool Regt.	27/06/1918	27/06/1918
Miscellaneous	Form Messages And Signals.		

17 KINGS LIVERPOOL

NOV 15 - JUNE 17

30TH DIVISION
89TH INFY BDE

17TH BN KING'S L'POOLS
NOV 1915 - JUN 1918

To UK

17 to dispatchers
vol. I

$\frac{121}{7624}$

Nov. 15.
June 1918.

I.C.
6 sheets

WAR DIARY 17th Bn King's Liverpool Regt
or
INTELLIGENCE SUMMARY

Army Form C. 2118.

(Erase heading not required.)

Instructions regarding War Diaries and Intelligence Summaries are contained in F. S. Regs., Part II. and the Staff Manual respectively. Title pages will be prepared in manuscript.

Hour, Date, Place	Summary of Events and Information	Remarks and references to Appendices
6 pm 8.11.15 LARK HILL CAMP SALISBURY PLAIN	MAJOR G.ROLLO, 2nd LIEUTS MARSHALL & LEWIS, 102 other ranks, 64 horses & mules and 19 wagons & carts left AMESBURY at 7.20 am for SOUTHAMPTON. BATMAN C.E.RYDER found shot at 6pm near STONEHENGE.	RGR
9 pm 9.11.15 OSTREHOVE CAMP BOULOGNE	The Left half Batt: left AMESBURY at 7/10 am arriving FOLKESTONE 12.20 pm the Right half Batt: arriving there shortly afterwards. The Batt: embarked on SS PRINCESS VICTORIA at 3pm arriving at BOULOGNE at 5 pm. On arrival, the Batt: marched to OSTREHOVE Rest camp. MAJOR ROLLO & transport arrived at HAVRE by SS NIRVANA at 10 a.m from SOUTHAMPTON, one mule died in transit.	RGR
6 pm 9.11.15 BELLANCOURT	The Batt: left OSTREHOVE Camp at 7.15 pm 8.11.15 and marched to GARE CENTRAL BOULOGNE Entraining there for PONT REMY (Left GARE CENTRAL at 8.30 pm arrived PONT REMY 12 midnight) On arrival at PONT REMY, Batt: marched to BELLANCOURT arriving 7 am 9.11.15 moving into Billets thereabouts 8.11.15. MAJOR ROLLO & Transport arrived BELLANCOURT at 1 pm On the eve. of departure for Active Service, a message from His Majesty THE KING dated 3 Nov 1915, was received, conveying His Majesty's heartfelt good wishes.	Reference Maps Sept 13 Sheet 12
" 10.11.15	Batt: in billets at BELLANCOURT wet weather	RGR
" 11.11.15	"	RGR
" 12.11.15	"	RGR
" 13.11.15	"	RGR
" 14.11.15	Fine during day, light snowfall during night	RGR
" 15.11.15	Fine weather	RGR
" 16.11.15	2r B.S Thompson was evacuated from BELLANCOURT to 98th Field Ambulance on medical grounds.	RGR

WAR DIARY
or
INTELLIGENCE SUMMARY

Army Form C. 2118.

17th Bn Kings Liverpool Regt

(Erase heading not required.)

Instructions regarding War Diaries and Intelligence Summaries are contained in F. S. Regs., Part II. and the Staff Manual respectively. Title pages will be prepared in manuscript.

Hour, Date, Place	Summary of Events and Information	Remarks and references to Appendices
7pm 17.11.15 SURCAMPS	Battalion left BELLANCOURT at 8.30 am, 17.11.15, and arrived at BRUCAMPS at 12 noon, where, after having had dinners, the Battalion split up, A & B Coys' transport & machine gun section proceeding to VAUCHELLES LES DOMARTS where they billeted (arrived at 1.30 pm) and C & D Coys & H.Q. proceeding to SURCAMPS where they arrived at 1.30 pm and moved into billets. Weather fine.	RGS
7pm 18.11.15 VIGNACOURT	A & B Coys, machine gunners & transport under Capt HIGGINS left VAUCHELLES LES DOMARTS at 8 am with orders to be at cross roads immediately east of 2nd S in SURCAMPS at 9 am where they arrived on time. H.Q., C & D Coys left SURCAMPS at 9 am & joined up with Capt Higgins at above mentioned cross roads. The Battalion then proceeded to VIGNACOURT via ST OUEN arriving at the outskirts of VIGNACOURT at 12.30 pm when dinners were partaken of; The Battalion moved into billets at VIGNACOURT at 1.30 pm. The condition of the road owing to frost made the transport question a difficult one but all obstacles were satisfactorily surmounted.	RGS

Army Form C. 2118.

17th Bn Kings Liverpool Regt

WAR DIARY
or
INTELLIGENCE SUMMARY

(Erase heading not required.)

Instructions regarding War Diaries and Intelligence Summaries are contained in F. S. Regs., Part II. and the Staff Manual respectively. Title pages will be prepared in manuscript.

Hour, Date, Place	Summary of Events and Information	Remarks and references to Appendices
7pm 19.11.15 VIGNACOURT	Batt in billets at VIGNACOURT. Cold, frosty weather	RGS
" 20.11.15 "	Bright, cold, frosty weather	RGS
" 21.11.15 "	Dull, cold weather.	RGS
	Extract from LONDON GAZETTE:- LPool: Temporary Captain to be Temporary Major, G. F. HIGGINS. To date 4.8.15.	
" 22.11.15 "	Batt in billets at VIGNACOURT. Dull, cold weather.	RGS
" 23.11.15 "	Fine. Draught mule received from A.S.C	RGS
" 24.11.15 "	Dull, misty.	RGS
" 25.11.15 "	Fine. The whole of D Coy threw one live bomb each (Mills No 5).	
" 26.11.15 "	Batt in billets of VIGNACOURT. Fine but coldish weather. The whole of B Coy threw one live bmb each (Mills No 5).	RGS
" 27.11.15 "	Batt in billets at VIGNACOURT. Fine frosty weather. Extract from Divl orders Part II No. Bare 20.11.15 "17/16124 R.S.M GOODMAN. H.V. appointed acting Quartermaster to date 7.11.15 vice Hon Lt & QM C.E. RYDER. Died 6.11.15	RGS
	17/16122 Coy S.M GRAY. W. appointed acting Regt Sgt Maj to date 7.11.15 vice R.S.M GOODMAN. H.V. appointed acting Q.M.	RGS

Army Form C. 2118.

17th Bn Kings Liverpool Regt

WAR DIARY
or
INTELLIGENCE SUMMARY
(Erase heading not required.)

Instructions regarding War Diaries and Intelligence Summaries are contained in F. S. Regs., Part II. and the Staff Manual respectively. Title pages will be prepared in manuscript.

Hour, Date, Place	Summary of Events and Information	Remarks and references to Appendices
7pm 28.11.15 BEAUMETZ SOMME	The Battalion left VIGNACOURT at 9.30 a.m. and marched via BERTEAUCOURT – DOMART-EN-PONTHIEU – RIBEAUCOURT to BEAUMETZ and PROUVILLE. B, C, D Coys and transport billeted at BEAUMETZ and A Coy and Machine Gun Section at PROUVILLE. The Battalion arrived at billets at 3 pm. Cold. Frosty weather. (References Sheet 5B 2.) E	Rcds Rcds Rcds
7pm 29.11.15	Battalion in billets at BEAUMETZ & PROUVILLE. Heavy rain.	
7pm 30.11.15	Battalion in billets at BEAUMETZ and PROUVILLE. Fine weather.	

2 C.
11 sheets

17th L'pool Rgt:-
Vol 2.

121/7834

30th K/[?]

CONFIDENTIAL

WAR DIARY

OF

17TH (SERVICE) BATT THE LIVERPOOL REGT

FROM 1.12.15 TO 31.12.15

(VOLUME II December 1915)

WAR DIARY
or
INTELLIGENCE SUMMARY

(Erase heading not required.)

Army Form C. 2118.

17th Bn King's Liverpool Regt

Instructions regarding War Diaries and Intelligence Summaries are contained in F.S. Regs., Part II. and the Staff Manual respectively. Title pages will be prepared in manuscript.

Hour, Date, Place	Summary of Events and Information	Remarks and references to Appendices
1.12.15 BEAUMETZ SOMME	Battalion in billets at BEAUMETZ and PROUVILLE. Weather dull but fine.	Reference Map Set 73 Sheet 12 AMIENS. RGS
2.12.15 — " —	Battalion in billets at BEAUMETZ and PROUVILLE. Heavy rain.	RGS
3.12.15 — " —	Battalion in billets at BEAUMETZ and PROUVILLE. Wet, dull weather.	RGS
4.12.15 — " —	Battalion in billets at BEAUMETZ and PROUVILLE. Wet, dull weather. Medical Officer's pony lost. Description:— Bay Gelding – white blaze face – white fetlock near fore – white stockings both hind – number of gov't K&R – number near fore 17.5.3.	RGS
5.12.15 — " —	Battalion in billets at BEAUMETZ & PROUVILLE. Fine morning, rain later.	RGS
6.12.15 — " —	Battalion in billets at BEAUMETZ & PROUVILLE. Mild changeable weather. M.O.'s pony found.	RGS
7.12.15 — " —	Battalion in billets at BEAUMETZ & PROUVILLE. Fine at first, rain later. 2nd Lt L.E. FAITHFULL appointments attached to 89th Inf'y Bde Headquarters as Assistant Staff Captain to date from 5th Dec 1915.	RGS

Army Form C. 2118.

17th Bn King's Liverpool Regt

WAR DIARY
or
INTELLIGENCE SUMMARY
(Erase heading not required.)

Instructions regarding War Diaries and Intelligence Summaries are contained in F. S. Regs., Part II. and the Staff Manual respectively. Title pages will be prepared in manuscript.

Hour, Date, Place	Summary of Events and Information	Remarks and references to Appendices
8.12.15 BEAUMETZ SOMME	Battalion in billets at BEAUMETZ & PROUVILLE. Mostly fine ½ time rain. A scheme for the improvement of billets in this Bn area was inaugurated in respect of sanitary arrangements etc. The main features of the scheme were the selection of a Coy HQ comprising (a) drying room (b) Coy store (c) Butchers shop (d) accomodation for personnel (abt 10) (e) Covered accomodation for travelling kitchen, the object being to centralise all the above at Coy HQ. A Bn workshop was also started and a site selected for a Bn bathing establishment. Appointed O.C. 73DE WORKSHOPS CAPT FRASER	RGS
9.12.15 "	Battalion in billets at BEAUMETZ & PROUVILLE. mild. Very wet.	RGS RGS
10.12.15 "	Battalion in billets at BEAUMETZ & PROUVILLE. Changeable weather	RGS
11.12.15 "	do Changeable weather	RGS
12.12.15 "	do Fine weather	RGS
	Extract from Bde letter B 292 T 11 "inst":- Lt L.E FAITHFUL and PTE WARRINER 73 Coy unit to be attached to Brigade Headquarters from Dec. 13 to 1915.	RGS
13.12.15 "	Battalion in billets at BEAUMETZ and PROUVILLE. Fine, frosty weather	RGS

Army Form C. 2118.

WAR DIARY
or
INTELLIGENCE SUMMARY
(Erase heading not required.)

17th Bn King's Liverpool Regt

Hour, Date, Place	Summary of Events and Information	Remarks and references to Appendices
14.12.15 BEAUMETZ SOMMES	Battalion in billets at BEAUMETZ and PROUVILLE. Fine, cold weather. DRO 830 dated 6th Dec :- Brigadier General F.A.G.Y. ELTON. R.A assumed Command of 30 Division from 2nd to 6th December 1915. Brigadier General F.J KEMPSTER. D.S.O took over the command of 30th Division from Brigadier General F.A.G.Y ELTON R.A from 6th Dec. 1915. DRO 871 dated 13th Dec 1915 :- Major General W.F.Y. C.VO C13 resumed command of 30th Division on December 12th 1915.	Rvs Rvs
15.12.15 BEAUMETZ SOMMES	Battalion in billets at BEAUMETZ & PROUVILLE. Wet, cold weather	
8.45am 16.12.15 BEAUMETZ Puchevillers	The Battalion left BEAUMETZ at 8.45 am and marched to PUCHEVILLERS via BERNAVILLE, FIENVILLERS, CANDAS, and VAL-DEMAISON, Fms DU ROSEL PUCHEVILLERS arriving in billets at 2.45 pm. Cold, misty weather. Condition of men rather bad, especially so from Fms DU ROSEL to PUCHEVILLERS.	
2.45pm PUCHEVILLERS	2nd LIEUT FARIS and 50 men remained at BEAUMETZ to carry on the work of improving the billets in BEAUMETZ & PROUVILLE. CAPT FRASER remained at BERNAVILLE in charge of 73DE WORKSHOPS. 1 Officer & 50 men from 18th Bn Manchester Regt & 1 Officer and 50 men from 19th Bn Manchester Regt were attached to this Bn, joining in at 3 pm at PUCHEVILLERS	Rvs

Army Form C. 2118.

17th Bn Kings Liverpool Regt

WAR DIARY
or
INTELLIGENCE SUMMARY
(Erase heading not required.)

Instructions regarding War Diaries and Intelligence Summaries are contained in F. S. Regs., Part II. and the Staff Manual respectively. Title pages will be prepared in manuscript.

Hour, Date, Place		Summary of Events and Information	Remarks and references to Appendices
5 pm	20.12.15 ENGLEBELMER	D Coy night digging under 2nd R.I.	
"	" MESNIL	B Coy night digging	
"	" HAMEL	1 man] A Coy wounded & evacuated to casualty clearing station. ✗ No 15106 Pte ECKROYD	✗ No 15106 Pte ECKROYD
		Wet, misty day	Rfs
4.30 pm	21.12.15 AUCHONVILLERS	C Coy left the trenches & returned to ENGLEBELMER	
5.30 pm	" ENGLEBELMER	D Coy went into trenches (left sector) 11th BDE near AUCHONVILLERS) under instruction] 7th 2nd R.I.	
"	" HAMEL	A Coy left the trenches & returned to billets at MESNIL	
5.15 pm	" MESNIL	B Coy went into trenches (right sector)] 11th Bde at HAMEL) under instruction] 1st EAST LANCS REGT.	Rfs
		Very wet weather.	
4.45 pm	22.12.15 ENGLEBELMER	C Coy night digging under 2nd R.I.	
5 pm	" MESNIL	A Coy night digging	Rfs
		Wet weather.	
5 pm	23.12.15 MESNIL	A Coy night digging	Rfs
		Fine weather.	

Army Form C. 2118.

1/7th Bn King's Liverpool Regt

WAR DIARY
or
INTELLIGENCE SUMMARY
(Erase heading not required.)

Instructions regarding War Diaries and Intelligence Summaries are contained in F.S. Regs., Part II. and the Staff Manual respectively. Title pages will be prepared in manuscript.

Hour, Date, Place	Summary of Events and Information	Remarks and references to Appendices
1.45 pm 24.12.15 AUCHONVILLERS	D Coy left trenches & returned to billets at ENGLEBELMER	RGS
24.12.15 HAMEL	B Coy left trenches & returned to billets at MESNIL. Mild, changeable weather	
9.30 am 25.12.15 ENGLEBELMER.	The Bn (plus detachment of 18th & 19th Manchesters) left ENGLEBELMER for PUCHEVILLERS.	RGS
3 pm " PUCHEVILLERS.	The Bn (plus detachments of 18th & 19th Manchesters) arrived in billets at PUCHEVILLERS. Changeable weather, some heavy rain.	RGS
9.30 am 26.12.15 PUCHEVILLERS	The Bn left PUCHEVILLERS for BEAUMETZ. Detachment of Manchester Regt proceeded to join their respective units independently.	RGS
4 pm 26.12.15 BEAUMETZ	Bn arrived in billets at BEAUMETZ & PROUVILLE. Fine weather. {BEAUMETZ} PROUVILLE	RGS
27.12.15 BEAUMETZ	Bn in billets at BEAUMETZ & PROUVILLE. Fine weather	RGS
28.12.15 "	Bn in billets at BEAUMETZ & PROUVILLE "	
29.12.15 "	Lt General CONGREVE inspected Bn billets	
1 pm 30.12.15	1 Officer & 16 men per Company left BEAUMETZ for Divl Grenade School at HALLOY LES PERNOIS for an 8 days course of instruction. Bn in billets at BEAUMETZ & PROUVILLE. Fine weather	RGS
1 pm 30.12.15		

1247 W 8299 200,000 (E) 8/14 J.B.C. &A. Forms/C. 2118/11.

Army Form C. 2118.

17th Bn King's Liverpool Regt

WAR DIARY
or
INTELLIGENCE SUMMARY
(Erase heading not required.)

Instructions regarding War Diaries and Intelligence Summaries are contained in F. S. Regs., Part II. and the Staff Manual respectively. Title pages will be prepared in manuscript.

Hour, Date, Place	Summary of Events and Information	Remarks and references to Appendices
31.12.15 BEAUMETZ	Bn in billets at BEAUMETZ & PROUVILLE	PG73 B.C. Fairfax; LIEUT. COL. 17TH (SERVICE) BATTN. THE LIVERPOOL REGIMENT 31.12.15

19th L'pool
Vol: 3
Jan 16.

B.C.
11 sheets

Sol: D:

Army Form C. 2118.

WAR DIARY
or
INTELLIGENCE SUMMARY

(Erase heading not required.)

Instructions regarding War Diaries and Intelligence Summaries are contained in F. S. Regs., Part II. and the Staff Manual respectively. Title pages will be prepared in manuscript.

Hour, Date, Place			Summary of Events and Information	Remarks and references to Appendices
	5.1.16	—	No 29669 Pte Simmons & No 23626 Pte Syfield evacuated to C.C.S	
9.30 am	5.1.16	NAOURS	Bn left NAOURS.	
3.15 pm	5.1.16	PONT NOYELLES	Bn arrived at PONT NOYELLES - fine weather	RBS
			2nd R Scots Fus billeted at LA HOUSSOYE & 200TH RE at PONT NOYELLES.	
9.30 am	6.1.16	PONT NOYELLES	Bn left PONT NOYELLES	
1.15 pm	6.1.16	SAILLY LORETTE	Bn arrived at SAILLY LORETTE. Changable weather	RBS
			2nd R Scots Fus billeted at ETINEHEM & CHIPILLY & 200TH RE at BRAY.	
3 pm	7.1.16	SAILLY LORETTE	Bn left SAILLY LORETTE	RBS
7.30 pm	7.1.16	SUZANNE	Bn arrived at SUZANNE. Fine at first, heavy rain later	
4.30 pm	8.1.16	SUZANNE	Bn left SUZANNE at 10 minutes interval between Coys & proceeded to MARICOURT to relieve 20TH BN K.L.R. in trenches Sector A4. This sector was in 14TH INFT BDE trench area & the Bn was, according, temporarily attached to this BDE (14TH).	
10.8 pm	8.1.16	MARICOURT Sector A4	Relief completed	
4 am	9.1.16	,,	A, B & C Coys in firing line reported situation normal D Coy in reserve in billets at MARICOURT	RBS

WAR DIARY
or
INTELLIGENCE SUMMARY
(Erase heading not required.)

Army Form C. 2118.

Instructions regarding War Diaries and Intelligence Summaries are contained in F.S. Regs., Part II. and the Staff Manual respectively. Title pages will be prepared in manuscript.

Hour, Date, Place	Summary of Events and Information	Remarks and references to Appendices
4.30 pm 9.1.16 MARICOURT Sector A4	Situation normal. Wind N.W. fine weather.	RGB I
4.30 am 10.1.16 —	Situation normal wind N.W slight	
4.30 pm 10.1.16 —	Situation normal except for some shelling of fire & support trenches in left subsector - wind south-west light.	
5.15 pm 10.1.16 MARICOURT DEFENCES	Bn took over MARICOURT defences from 16th Manchesters	
6.35 pm 10.1.16 —	Relief of Bn by 20th L'POOLS in Sector A4 completed.	RGB
10.1.16 —	No 21979 Pte RALPH evacuated to CCS	
4.30 am 11.1.16 —	Situation normal	
10.30 am 11.1.16 —	Some shelling of X roads A22.a.34 and N.S. no damage	
3.10 pm 11.1.16 —	About 20 shells fell in MARICOURT tonight. no casualties (2nd Lt R.H SMITH wounded) Wind N.W.	
4.30 am 12.1.16 MARICOURT SECTOR A4	Situation normal.	
3 pm 12.1.16 —	Bn started to relieve 20TH L'POOLS in Trenches Sector A4	
5 pm 12.1.16 —	Relief completed & MARICOURT DEFENCES handed over to 20TH L'POOLS.	RGB.
4.30 pm 12.1.16 —	Situation normal.	
4.30 am 13.1.16 —	Situation normal.	
4.30 am 13.1.16 —	Shelling) Trenches continued from morn. Lit without any Wind N.W. fine but squally.	
4.30 pm 13.1.16 —	damage)	
— 13.1.16	No 23626 Pte JYFIELD returned from CCS.	RGB
4.30 am 13.1.16	Capt B STERN left for BRAY to report to Town Major for instruction	
2 am 14.1.16 —	Situation - Some shelling during the night of communication Trenches in subsector 28, 29 & 30. Wind N.	
2 am 14.1.16 —	No 16050 Pte BROWNLEE. L.C (D Coy), No 15563 Pte Roberts Rein (C Coy) & No 24934 Pte Harvey C.E (D Coy) accidentally killed by premature explosion of rifle grenade	

WAR DIARY
or
INTELLIGENCE SUMMARY
(Erase heading not required.)

Army Form C. 2118.

Instructions regarding War Diaries and Intelligence Summaries are contained in F. S. Regs., Part II. and the Staff Manual respectively. Title pages will be prepared in manuscript.

Hour, Date, Place			Summary of Events and Information	Remarks and references to Appendices
4 pm	14.1.16	MARICOURT Sector A4	Situation - considerable shelling of trenches. Wind N, fine.	
8.30 pm	14.1.16	"	No 15887 Pte M Guthrie died of wounds	RGS
	14.1.16	"	About 50 77 millimetre shells fell within 100 to 300 yards of A22a 0/5	
4 am	15.1.16	"	No 15360 Pte W.D. Rowlands evacuated to CCS	RGS
3 pm	15.1.16	"	Situation normal - wind light SW.	
4 am	16.1.16	"	Heavy shelling of light and left subsector fire and communication trench between 2 & 3 pm. Wind NW	
4 pm	16.1.16	"	Situation normal - wind NW	
	16.1.16	"	Situation normal, heavy shelling of track leading to SUZANNE S of Bn HQ - Wind N.W.	RGS
5 pm	16.1.16	"	20TH Bn KLR started to relieve 17TH KLR in Sector A4	
10 pm	16.1.16	"	Relief completed	
12 am	17.1.16	SUZANNE	Bn arrived at SUZANNE & went into rest billets.	
	17.1.17	"	Bn in billets at SUZANNE. 2nd Lt LAWRENCE transferred to 4TH Bn LPOOL REGT. Dull rainy weather	RGS
	18.1.17	"	Bn in billets at SUZANNE. Dull rainy weather	RGS
	19.1.17	"	Fine weather	RGS
	20.1.17	"	1 mule killed by a shell & 1 riding horse wounded.	
5 pm	20.1.17	MARICOURT A4	Bn started to relieve 20= LPOOLS	
7.12 pm	20.1.17	"	Relief completed	
4.30 am	21.1.17	"	Situation normal. Wind West.	RGS

Army Form C. 2118.

WAR DIARY
or
INTELLIGENCE SUMMARY

(Erase heading not required.)

Instructions regarding War Diaries and Intelligence Summaries are contained in F. S. Regs., Part II. and the Staff Manual respectively. Title pages will be prepared in manuscript.

Hour, Date, Place	Summary of Events and Information	Remarks and references to Appendices
4 pm 21.1.16 MARICOURT SECTOR A4	Situation normal, Wind S.W.	Refs
4 am 22.1.16	do	
4 pm 22.1.16	Situation severe shelling of trenches 33, 34 & 35 by whizz bangs. Bombardment casualties O.R. 2 killed and 1 wounded.	Refs
4 am 23.1.16	Wind S.W. Situation normal, wind S.W.	Refs
3.50 pm 23.1.16	Situation normal. Some rifle grenades thrown into A.P.1. Wind S.E. Casualties - 1 O.R. wounded by rifle grenade	
4 am 24.1.16	Situation normal	
3.30 pm 24.1.16	Situation normal S.W. Casualties O.R. 1 killed & 1 slightly wounded.	
9.35 pm 24.1.16	20th L.Pools completed relief of 17th L.Pools in A4	Refs
9.30 pm 24.1.16 MARICOURT DEFENCES	17th L.Pools completed relief of 2nd R.S.FUS in MARICOURT DEFENCES	
3.30 am 25.1.16	Situation normal. Wind S.W.	Fine weather
4 pm 25.1.16	do	"
4 am 26.1.16	do	
4 pm 26.1.16	do	
12.15 pm 26.1.16	Gas helmet test	
26.1.16	Casualties O.R. 1 slightly wounded by Art. fire	Refs
4 am 27.1.16	Situation normal, Wind S.W.	
4 pm 27.1.16	do	
27.1.16	Casualties - O.R. 2 wounded	Refs
3.30 am 28.1.16	Situation normal Wind S.W.	

Army Form C. 2118.

WAR DIARY
or
INTELLIGENCE SUMMARY

(Erase heading not required.)

Instructions regarding War Diaries and Intelligence Summaries are contained in F. S. Regs., Part II. and the Staff Manual respectively. Title pages will be prepared in manuscript.

Hour, Date, Place	Summary of Events and Information	Remarks and references to Appendices
6.30 am 28.1.16 MARICOURT DEFENCES	Heavy bombardment by our guns, apparently on villages in rear of enemy lines.	
7.30 am " "	Enemy retaliation on our batteries – heavy shelling	
9.45 am " "	Apparent enemy shelling SUZANNE with lachrymatory shells which continued intermittently till about 4 pm	
11.10 am " "	Very heavy shelling of MARICOURT by enemy (abt 1000 shells). Bombardment continued till 12.30 pm. Relief of 20TH 2POSTS in Subsector A4 by 17TH 4POSTS suspended.	
12.30 pm " "	Barrage placed across MARICOURT – SUZANNE RD and across valley lying between MARICOURT and SUZANNE by enemy, which barrage was kept up till 5.30 pm (1½ Coys 17TH M'TERS arrived in support of MARICOURT DEFENCES)	
12.37 pm " "	Order received from 90TH BDE to man MARICOURT DEFENCES	
2 pm " "	Telegram despatched to 90TH BDE to the effect that MARICOURT DEFENCES were manned.	
3.30 pm " "	Intermittent enemy bombardment of "S" works, MARICOURT DEFENCES, which extended till about 5.30 pm.	
6.30 pm " "	Cessation of enemy artillery activity. Casualties – OR 2 Killed, 5 wounded	

Army Form C. 2118.

WAR DIARY
or
INTELLIGENCE SUMMARY
(Erase heading not required.)

Instructions regarding War Diaries and Intelligence Summaries are contained in F. S. Regs., Part II. and the Staff Manual respectively. Title pages will be prepared in manuscript.

Hour, Date, Place	Summary of Events and Information	Remarks and references to Appendices
4 am 29.1.16 MARICOURT DEFENCES	Situation normal wind nil	
6.30 am — „ —	GAS message received. The gas attack was on 21st BDE and actual effects were not felt at MARICOURT	RRS
3.40 pm — „ —	Situation normal – Wind S. Evacuation to CCS during week ending 29.1.16 OR 3	RRS
3.30 am 30.1.16	Situation normal, Wind E	
3.30 pm 30.1.16	Situation normal, Wind NE	
3.45 am 31.1.16	Situation normal, Wind NE	
12 pm 31.1.16	Enemy put about 100 Rifle into MARICOURT between 12 pm & 12.30 pm	
4 pm 31.1.16	Situation normal. Wind SW	RRS

B.C. Fawcus
LIEUT. COLONEL
COMM 1/7th (GERRARD BATH THE LIVERPOOL REGT)

31.1.16

CONFIDENTIAL

WAR DIARY OF 17TH BN LIVERPOOL REGT

VOLUME IV FROM 1-2-16 TO 29-2-16.

WAR DIARY
or
INTELLIGENCE SUMMARY
(Erase heading not required.)

Army Form C. 2118.

Instructions regarding War Diaries and Intelligence Summaries are contained in F. S. Regs., Part II. and the Staff Manual respectively. Title pages will be prepared in manuscript.

Hour, Date, Place			Summary of Events and Information	Remarks and references to Appendices
3.30 am	1.2.16	MARICOURT DEFENCES	Situation normal - Wind NW	RAS
3.30 pm	1.2.16	"	Situation normal - Wind SW.	
3.30 am	2.2.16	"	Situation normal - Wind nil	
9 am	2.2.16	"	Bn commenced to relieve 20th L'pools in Sector A4	
10.40 am	2.2.16	SECTOR A4 MARICOURT	Relief completed	RAS
3.10 pm	2.2.16	"	Situation normal - Wind SE	
3.30 am	3.2.16	"	Situation normal - Wind SE	RAS
4 pm	3.2.16	"	Enemy shelled firing & commn unication Trenches	
6 pm	3.2.16	"	Situation normal - Wind S	
3.40 am	4.2.16	"	Situation - some shelling of MARICOURT VILLAGE by 77 mm guns, Wind S.	
3.45 pm	4.2.16	"	Some 300 shells, mostly 77 mm, some 4.2 & 5.9 fell in MARICOURT AVENUE and MARICOURT VILLAGE between 6 pm & 6.30 pm (Lt. H.G. WAINWRIGHT) 1 Officer & 50 OR wounded.	RAS
6 pm	4.2.16	"	Situation now normal - Wind SW.	
3.30 am	5.2.16	"		
4 pm	5.2.16	"	Situation normal, Wind W-SW	RAS
3.30 am	6.2.16	"	Situation normal, Wind SW	

WAR DIARY
or
INTELLIGENCE SUMMARY

(Erase heading not required.)

Army Form C. 2118.

Instructions regarding War Diaries and Intelligence Summaries are contained in F. S. Regs., Part II. and the Staff Manual respectively. Title pages will be prepared in manuscript.

Hour, Date, Place	Summary of Events and Information	Remarks and references to Appendices
3.30 pm 6.2.16 Sub Sector A4 MARICOURT	20 L'POORS started to relieve 17TH L'POORS in A4 SUBSECTOR	
3 pm 6.2.16	Situation determined shelling of village all day with 4.2 & whizz bangs from N.E. & East - Wind S.E.	
9.30 pm 6.2.16 MARICOURT DEFENCES	MARICOURT DEFENCES manned by 1 Coy 20TH L'POORS, 2 Coys 17TH MANCHESTERS & A & B Coys 17TH L'POORS	
	C Coy 17TH L'POORS remained in reserve in A4 & D Coy 17TH L'POORS moved to SUZANNE	
4 pm 7.2.16	Coy of Royal Dragoons engaged on repairing of Royal Dragoons	
10.a.m 7.2.16	C Coy 17TH L'POORS relieved C Coy 20TH L'POORS in U works. MAJOR ROWE took over command of 17TH L'POORS	
4 pm 7.2.16	2 BEDFORDS began relief of 17TH L'POORS in MARICOURT DEFENCES. The 2 Coys 17TH MANCHESTERS which were in HQ & about Coy 17TH L'POORS. moved to SUZANNE & about Coy 17TH L'POORS. B Coy 17TH L'POORS remained at MARICOURT DEFENCES. A Coy 17TH L'POORS sent 2 platoon under MAJOR HIGGINS to A2 & 2 platoon under MR PORRITT to Battle dugouts West of VAUX WOOD. D Coy 17TH L'POORS moved from SUZANNE to Royal Dragoons	

WAR DIARY
or
INTELLIGENCE SUMMARY

(Erase heading not required.)

Army Form C. 2118.

Instructions regarding War Diaries and Intelligence Summaries are contained in F.S. Regs., Part II. and the Staff Manual respectively. Title pages will be prepared in manuscript.

Hour, Date, Place	Summary of Events and Information	Remarks and references to Appendices
4.30 pm 8.2.16 SUZANNE	Heavy enemy shelling of SUZANNE from EAST	RHB
6.30 pm 9.2.16	2 Platoon C Coy started to relieve 2 platoon of A Coy in A 2 Subsector. The 2 A Coy retired.	
8 pm 9.2.16	2 Platoon J A Coy arrived at SUZANNE from A 2 subsector.	
8.30 pm 9.2.16	2 Platoon C Coy started to relieve 2 Platoon A Coy in Bois d'en VAUX WOOD	RBS
10.30 pm 9.2.16	2 Platoon A Coy arrived at SUZANNE from VAUX WOOD	RCB
12.45 am 10.2.16	Heavy enemy shelling of SUZANNE. Enemy shelling ceased.	RHB
1.30 am 10.2.16		
3 pm 11.2.16 A 4	Relief of 20 Zepoors in A 4 commenced	
6.50 am 12.2.16	Relief completed. Situation normal – Wind N.W.	
3.25 pm 12.2.16	Adjutant left for FRIXECOURT to go through course at 3rd Army Infantry School.	RHB
5 pm 12.2.16		
3.30 am 13.2.16	Situation normal – wind slight S.W.	

WAR DIARY
or
INTELLIGENCE SUMMARY
(Erase heading not required.)

Army Form C. 2118.

Instructions regarding War Diaries and Intelligence Summaries are contained in F.S. Regs., Part II. and the Staff Manual respectively. Title pages will be prepared in manuscript.

Hour, Date, Place	Summary of Events and Information	Remarks and references to Appendices
4 pm. 13/2/16 At SUBSECTOR	Situation normal – wind S.W. – Col. Fanfan left for 3rd Army School at FLIXECOURT.	RGS.
3.30 am 14/2/16	do	
4 pm 14/2/16	Situation normal – wind S.W.	RSS
3 am 15/2/16	Situation normal – wind S.W.	
4 pm 15/2/16	Situation normal – wind West	
3 am 16/2/16	Situation normal – wind S.W.	
4 pm 16/2/16	Situation normal – wind West	
noon 16/2/16	Bn came under orders of 89th Bde.	
4 pm 16/2/16	Relief by 20th Sport started	EOTS
12 pm 16/2/16	Relief completed	
4 am 17/2/16 BRAY	Bn arrived & billets at BRAY	
10 am 18/2/16	Bn left BRAY for DAOURS less 2/Lt Blakey & 30 O.R. sent to GUILLAUCOURT, Capt Robinson 2/Lt Sprowt & 2/Lt Johnston & 130 O.R. sent to LES ETANGS CORBIE & Capt Irwin 2/Lt Paris 2/Lt Bellow & 100 O.R. sent to LONGPRÉS all on working parties	RGB
6 pm 18/2/16 DAOURS	Bn arrived at DAOURS.	NSS.
19/2/16	Bn in billets at DAOURS. Working party of 6 Offrs & 300 men supplied to work on DAOURS CONTAY line under orders 110th Fd Coy RE VECQUEMONT	

1247 W 3299 200,000 (E) 8/14 J.B.C.&A. Forms/C. 2118/11.

WAR DIARY
or
INTELLIGENCE SUMMARY

(Erase heading not required.)

Army Form C. 2118.

Hour, Date, Place	Summary of Events and Information	Remarks and references to Appendices
20/2/16 DAOURS	Bn - billets at DAOURS. Fine weather. Working party supplied as yesterday	RWS
21/2/16 —	Bn in billets at DAOURS - Fine weather working party again supplied in morning	RWS
22/2/16 —	Bn in billets at DAOURS. Fine weather working party 300 men & 6 offrs supplied to 110 Coy RE VECQUEMONT	RWS
23.2.16 —	Bn in billets at DAOURS - Same working party as previously	RWS
24.2.16 —	Bn in billets at DAOURS. Snow fell	RWS
25.2.16 —	—	RWS
11.30 am 26.2.16 CORBIE	Bn left DAOURS.	RWS
1.45 pm —	Vaux working party joined up with Bn	
6 pm — ETINEHEM	Bn arrived at ETINEHEM CAMP	
8 pm —	LONGORE's working party arrived ETINEHEM CAMP	RWS
27.2.16 —	Bn in billets at ETINEHEM	RWS
1 am 28.2.16 —	Bn left ETINEHEM to relieve 1/7 Gordons in A1 subsector MARICOURT	
6.30 am 28.2.16 A1 SUBSECTOR MARICOURT	Relief complete	RWS

Army Form C. 2118.

WAR DIARY
or
INTELLIGENCE SUMMARY
(Erase heading not required.)

Instructions regarding War Diaries and Intelligence Summaries are contained in F. S. Regs., Part II. and the Staff Manual respectively. Title pages will be prepared in manuscript.

Hour, Date, Place	Summary of Events and Information	Remarks and references to Appendices
3.30 am 29.2.16 A1.SUBSECTR MARICOURT	Situation normal wind S.E	
3.30 pm —	Situation normal wind EAST	Rets

B.C. Jenkin
B. 17. G. King's Reg.
M. Clard.
Come S. 17. G. King's Reg.

17th Liverpool Vol 5

5 C.
5 sheet

Army Form C. 2118.

WAR DIARY
or
INTELLIGENCE SUMMARY
(Erase heading not required.)

Instructions regarding War Diaries and Intelligence Summaries are contained in F. S. Regs., Part II. and the Staff Manual respectively. Title pages will be prepared in manuscript.

Hour, Date, Place			Summary of Events and Information	Remarks and references to Appendices
	1.3.16	A1 MARICOURT	Bn in Trenches	R.L.B
	2.3.16	Z.1 MARICOURT	Name of subsector occupied changed from A1 to Z1	R.L.B
8.45 pm	—	—	Relief by 19th L'Pools commenced.	R.L.B
10 pm	—	—	A Coy relieved one Coy 2nd BEDFORDS in V works	R.L.B
1.20 am	3.3.16	—	Relief by 19th L'Pools Complete.	
5 am	3.3.16	ETINEHEM	Bn less A Coy arrived in billets	
	4.3.16	—	Bn at ETINEHEM	9PRB gPRB
	5.3.16	—	—	
5 pm	5.3.16	—	Bn left ETINEHEM to relieve 19th L'POOLS in Z1	9PRB
1.20 am	6.3.16	Z1	Relief complete.	9PRB
7.15 pm	8.3.16	Z1	19th L'Pools started to relieve 17th L'POOLS	9PRB
8.45 pm	8.3.16	Z1	Relief complete 17 L'Pools moved to MARICOURT DEFENCES	
	9.3.16	MARICOURT DEFENCES	Bn in MARICOURT DEFENCES	9PRB
	10.3.16	—	—	9PRB
	11.3.16	—	—	9PRB
7.15 pm	12.3.16	—	Bn commenced relief of 19th L'POOLS in Z1	9PRB
8.45 pm	12.3.16	Z1	Relief complete	9PRB

Army Form C. 2118.

WAR DIARY
or
INTELLIGENCE SUMMARY

(Erase heading not required.)

Instructions regarding War Diaries and Intelligence Summaries are contained in F.S. Regs., Part II. and the Staff Manual respectively. Title pages will be prepared in manuscript.

Hour, Date, Place		Summary of Events and Information	Remarks and references to Appendices
	13.3.16	Z1	Bn in Z1 subsector	Appx.
	14.3.16	Z1	do	Appx.
9 pm		Z1	Enemy put about 300 shells into MARICOURT village.	
9 pm	15.3.16	Z1	S. Staffords commenced to relieve Bn in Z1. Some enemy shelling.	Appx.
1.15 am	16.3.16	Z1	Relief complete	Appx.
3.30 am	16.3.16	Z1	Bn arrived at Grovetown Camp Bray	Appx.
5.15 am	17.3.16	Grovetown Camp	Bn left camp & proceeded to CORBIE	Appx.
10.30 am	17.3.16	CORBIE	Bn arrived at CORBIE & billeted in B area.	Appx.
9 am	18.3.16	—	Bn left CORBIE for FRANVILLERS	Appx.
10.30 am	—	FRANVILLERS	Bn arrived FRANVILLERS.	Appx.
	19.3.16	—	Bn in billets at FRANVILLERS.	Appx.
	20.3.16	—	do	Appx.
	21.3.16	—	"	Appx.
	22.3.16	—	"	Appx.
	23. " "	—	"	Appx.
	24. " "	—	"	Appx.
	25. " "	—	"	Appx.
	26. " "	—	"	Appx.
	27. " "	—	"	Appx.

WAR DIARY
or
INTELLIGENCE SUMMARY

Army Form C. 2118.

Hour, Date, Place	Summary of Events and Information	Remarks and references to Appendices
8.30 a.m. 28th FRANVILLERS	Bn. left for ETINEHEM CAMP; owing to some enemy shelling delayed outside ETINEHEM, proceeding by Platoons arrived at 1.45 p.m.	appx.
29th ETINEHEM CAMP	Bn. at CAMP. Working party 50 men under Lt. Parritt to MERICOURT LOCK; 2 OR work in ETINEHEM.	appx.
30th "	" ETINEHEM out of bounds on account of MEASLES.	appx.
31st "	Above parties + in addition 50 OR under Lt BOUNDY to ETINEHEM CREEK; R. employed in building huts in camp for kitchens & building new Latrines.	appx.

B. Hanbury LIEUT. COL:
17TH (SERVICE) BATT. THE LIVERPOOL REGIMENT

17 Liverpool Vol 6

CONFIDENTIAL.

WAR DIARY
of
17th BATTALION KING'S LIVERPOOL REGIMENT

(VOLUME 6.)

from 1st April 1916 to 30th April 1916.

Army Form C. 2118.

WAR DIARY
or
INTELLIGENCE SUMMARY
(Erase heading not required.)

Instructions regarding War Diaries and Intelligence Summaries are contained in F. S. Regs., Part II. and the Staff Manual respectively. Title pages will be prepared in manuscript.

Hour, Date, Place	Summary of Events and Information	Remarks and references to Appendices
Apl 1st ETINEHEM CAMP.	Major ROLLO & Lt RODNEY returned from leave.	
" 2nd "	2. Mr GOODMAN & 2nd Lt MARSHALL went on leave.	
" 3rd "	1 Platoon under 2nd Lt BLABEY as working party for GUILLACOURT, transferring road metal, platoon under Lgt Williams to work railhead CORBIE. A Coy under Capt Torrey to MARICOURT. 5 p.m to work on defences. Reinforcement of five officers, viz Capt. C.E. TORREY 2nd Lt. R.V. MERRY J.G. DIXON A.E. BAGNALL & P.L. WRIGHT. joined on the night 2/3rd Aplt. General MAXSE cmdg 18th Div. visited Etinehem Camp & expressed his approval of work done there by this Bn. C.O. went on leave. Major Rolls in command.	A Coy returned Camp evg to outbreak of measles.
" 4th ETINEHEM CAMP.	Work in Camp.	
" 5th "	2nd Lt Brinsen & 2. Lt Draper went on leave D Coy under Lt Wilson & 2nd Lt WRIGHT relieves A Coy at MARICOURT & A Coy isolated in CAMP. Capt Baugh returned from leave.	
" 6th "		
" 7th "		
" 8th "		
" 9th "		
" 10th "		
" 11th "	Work in Camp.	
" 12th "		
" 13th "		
" 14th "		

WAR DIARY
or
INTELLIGENCE SUMMARY
(Erase heading not required.)

Army Form C. 2118.

Instructions regarding War Diaries and Intelligence Summaries are contained in F. S. Regs., Part II. and the Staff Manual respectively. Title pages will be prepared in manuscript.

Hour, Date, Place	Summary of Events and Information	Remarks and references to Appendices
15th to 28th April ETINEHEM CAMP	Bn in camp	
29th April	Working parties supplied the Bn	
6.30pm 30th April	Bn left ETINEHEM camp to relieve 8" Norfolks in Z1 subsector	
11.15pm Z1	Relief complete	

B C Fawkes
LIEUT COL
17TH (SERVICE) BATT: THE LIVERPOOL REGIMENT

17 Liverpool Vol. 7

CONFIDENTIAL

War Diary
of
17th (Ser) Bn. The King's (Liverpool Regt.)

from 1.5.1916. to. 31.5.1916.

Volume VII.

Army Form C. 2118.

WAR DIARY
or
INTELLIGENCE SUMMARY
(Erase heading not required.)

Instructions regarding War Diaries and Intelligence Summaries are contained in F.S. Regs, Part II. and the Staff Manual respectively. Title pages will be prepared in manuscript.

Hour, Date, Place			Summary of Events and Information	Remarks and references to Appendices
12 mg/ns	21		Situation normal	
1.45 am	5 May	21	Heavy enemy shelling on ROUND POINT aunt	
2.30	"	"	A 17/3, 4 & 5.	
			Enemy bombardment ceased – no damage sustained	
8 am	"	"	19th Kings started to relieve us	
9.10	"	"	Relief complete	
10 pm	"	"	The Bn took over MARICOURT DEFENCES	
6 am ⎫ MARICOURT			The Bn furnished all available men for	
7 am ⎪			work lines R.E. on the various Regt &	
8 am ⎬ DEFENCES			Supporting points in the Defences. Trenches	
9 am ⎭			were deepened, fire bays & steps constructed	
			& wire put up	
11 am	10 May	—	Our position bombarded every front line	
			with 18 pounders, 8 inch & 4.5 inch how/rs	
2 pm	"	—	Enemy retaliated by shelling MARICOURT	
			& continued till about 4.30 pm – no	
			damage sustained	

Army Form C. 2118.

WAR DIARY
or
INTELLIGENCE SUMMARY
(Erase heading not required.)

Instructions regarding War Diaries and Intelligence Summaries are contained in F.S. Regs., Part II. and the Staff Manual respectively. Title pages will be prepared in manuscript.

Hour, Date, Place			Summary of Events and Information	Remarks and references to Appendices
5pm	11.5.16	MAILCOURT DEFENCES	Bn started to relieve 18-KRR in 21	
5.40pm	"	21	Relief complete	
7.45pm	"	21	Enemy shelled front line trenches A17/1, A17/2, A17/3, A17/4 for about 3/4 hour. Rear by u.b. 4.5, 5.9 & minenwerfer — shells came from NORTH. Support & communication trenches were also shelled with 4.5 & 18 pdrs. Our Artillery replied with — 2nd Lt DAKIN wounded. 5 OR killed 9 " wounded	
1am	13.5.16	21	Heavy enemy artillery fire chiefly directed on the sector on our right (Y3) where an attack was made & repulsed. Our trenches were shelled with minenwerfer 4.2's, whizzbangs, in addition to battery replies. Difficult. 1 O/R (at BAGNAUX) 1 OR wounded	
3am	13.5.16	21	Situation quiet	
9.30pm	17.5.16	21	19-KRR commenced to relieve us in 21	
11.45pm	"	—	Relief complete — B9C Fazenia went to TRIGGER WOOD — 2 platoons D Coy to SUZANNE & remainder D Coy of A Coy to ERINGHEM CASUALTIES 2/Lt 170 Pte Perry EQ 3 wounded by artillery fire 17/5/1815 L/Cpt Francon P3	

Forms/C. 2118/11.

WAR DIARY or INTELLIGENCE SUMMARY

Army Form C. 2118.

(Erase heading not required.)

Instructions regarding War Diaries and Intelligence Summaries are contained in F. S. Regs., Part II. and the Staff Manual respectively. Title pages will be prepared in manuscript.

Hour, Date, Place	Summary of Events and Information	Remarks and references to Appendices
18.5.16 ETINEHEM	Bn billeted as on the 17th. Detachment at Lagarm 2 Lt Whyte went out at night with R.E. to Edand Flank CHIPILLY	
19 "	Bn in billets as above	
20 "	" " "	
21 "	" " "	
22 "	" " "	
23.5.16 ETINEHEM	Bn moved to CORBIE via horse race road. Billeted in 'C' area CORBIE, arrived in billets 9.20pm	
24.5.16	Left ETINEHEM 5.0pm. Relieved by 5 Bn Norfolks. Bn left for VAUX-EN-AMIENOIS at 4.8am arrived in billets there in area W of road running N.O.S. east of Church. Arrived in billets 10.15 ¾ am	
25.5.16 VAUX-EN-AMIENOIS	Bn in billets. Lt T.B. Wilkin RAMC attached 98th field Ambulance	
26.5.16	FGCM on 17/26172 Pte W. Lawton Kell Bn to S. Ho VAUX-ENAMIENOIS Charge 22/5/16. When on active service refusing to perform active service. Keying on rest post AA See 6 (1K) Plea - Not Guilty. Finding Hn East - Guilty. 3 Years P.S. Sentence. Confirmed. J.C. Nicolai Brig Gen. 81st Bgd Bde 22.5.16 Sentence Major G.P. Hyde Q. LT ORR RAME attached vice LT Dawson to 98 FA	

Forms/C. 2118/11.

17th Kings L.Pool

June
1916

Army Form C. 2118.

WAR DIARY
OR
INTELLIGENCE SUMMARY
(Erase heading not required.)

1/7th Bn. King's Liverpool Regt.

Hour, Date, Place	Summary of Events and Information	Remarks and references to Appendices
1st – 10th June VAUX-EN-AMIENOIS	Bn. & Brigade training in attack on German trenches opposite 22 Subsector (AP3 to HEAD ST)	
11th June 11am	Trial Brigade attack 13th Corps 7th Bde Commanders & some French officers were present	
9.30 am 12th June	Bn. left VAUX and entrained at AILLY-SUR-SOMME	
3.30 pm HEILLY	Bn. arrived at HEILLY & detrained	
7.50 pm 15th June BRAY	Bn. arrived at BRAY having marched from Heilly. Major G. ROSE, 16122 R.S.M. GRAY W. and 15284 Sgt. STIRLING D. (master cook) mentioned in Sir Douglas Haig's despatches.	
9.30 pm 17th June BRAY	Bn. left BRAY to relieve 17th Manchesters in MARICOURT DEFENCES	
12.30 am 18 June MARICOURT DEFENCES	Relief complete	
24 June	"U" day – our artillery bombard enemy along whole front to be attacked.	
25 Jun	"V" day – bombardment continued – enemy's French mortars taking considerable part. Wnd. R.G. HEAP and 38 O.R. arrived at BRAY from line on Stmpt. K.	
26 Jun	"W" day – Team bombardment of enemy system continued. Bn. relieved 2nd Bn. Bedfordshire Regt. in Z.2. sub-sector.	

WAR DIARY
or
INTELLIGENCE SUMMARY

(Erase heading not required.)

Army Form C. 2118.

Hour, Date, Place	Summary of Events and Information	Remarks and references to Appendices
night 26th/27th June contd.	Heavy enemy bombardment of front line trenches. Casualties - killed OR 17, wounded OR 57	
27th June	"X" Day - Heavy bomb and ment continued by our artillery. weather became very bad, much rain falling, rendering the trenches very difficult.	
28th June	"Y" Day - Bombardment continued. Enemy reply on our front trenches continued. Casualties OR killed 3, wounded OR 15. Wet weather continued. "Z" day postponed 48 hours. that account	
29th June	Our artillery bombardment continued but less severe. weather somewhat clearer.	
30th June	Bombardment continued heavily. weather fine - trenches much improved.	

Ge Rolls Major & Lt Col.
Cmdg 17 Kings Lpool Rgt

War Diary

of

17th Bn. King's (Liverpool) Regt.

for

July 1916.

89/30 30 July
17 Liverpools
Vol 9

9C
12 sheets

CONFIDENTIAL

WAR DIARY

OF

17TH BN: KING'S (LIVERPOOL) REGIMENT

FROM 1ST JULY 1916 TO 31ST JULY 1916

VOLUME 9.

Army Form C. 2118.

WAR DIARY
or
INTELLIGENCE SUMMARY
(Erase heading not required.)

Instructions regarding War Diaries and Intelligence Summaries are contained in F. S. Regs., Part II. and the Staff Manual respectively. Title pages will be prepared in manuscript.

Hour, Date, Place	Summary of Events and Information	Remarks and references to Appendices
3.30 a.m. 7.7.16 Z2 Subsect	Bn in position in assembly trenches - stances spread in quarters Bn frontage from MARICOURT-MAMETZ RD to 100 yds west of MARICOURT-MONTAUBAN RD. 1st wave 2 platoons A Cy on the right & 2 platoon B Cy on the left - 2nd wave now consists of three companies - 3rd wave C Cy & 4 guns (D Cy) - pressed route at about 100 yds intervals. 3rd Bn 153rd Regt. French infantry on our right 9.20 Tr. K.L.R on our left. The objective was DUBLIN TRENCH from DUBLIN REDOUBT exclusive to a point 400 yds west.	Reference map MONTAUBAN 1/10,000
7.30 a.m. — —	"zero hour" the assault commenced, some shelling but very slight infantry resistance & but little machine gun fire encountered. The work of our artillery has been very effective on the German Trenches.	
8.30 a.m. — —	The objective was taken at 8.30 a.m. the French on our right gaining their's at the same & ours. Lt. Col. J. C. BRADFORD Commandant LE PETIT commg 3rd Bn 153rd Regt arrived together in DUBLIN TRENCH Nº 73 Boy dug in about 100 yds North of DUBLIN TRENCH which the Germans shelled intermittently all day but not heavily touching the new trench much. Casualties 7 to 12 noon CAPT E.C. TORREY commg C Cy. 2 LT D.M. SCOTT commg A Cy & 2 LT P.L. WRIGHT wounded.	
12 noon — —	100 O.R.	

WAR DIARY
or
INTELLIGENCE SUMMARY
(Erase heading not required.)

Army Form C. 2118.

Hour, Date, Place	Summary of Events and Information	Remarks and references to Appendices
9 pm 3/7/16 DUBLIN TRENCH	2nd Dublin Bn attacked BERNAFAY WOOD Successfully. Bn Lieutenants 2 Lts M.J. CRAIG, J.M. MORRIS, S.J. IRELAND, J.F.W. BERRY, D.M. RIDDELL, J.R. MICHAELIS. Philo, and come up to FAVIERE SUPPORT & G.S. way in last line to MONTAUBAN. Casualties killed OR 8 wounded OR 24	R. MICHAELIS.
3.30 pm 4. 7.16 —do—	1st 4th Bn South African Infy started to relieve us. Casualties OR killed 3, wounded 4.	
2 am 5. 7.16 —do—	Relief complete, platoon in relieved march up to BOIS DES TAILLES	
6.7.16 BOIS DES TAILLES	Day spent in rest. Bn billeted at CHIPILLY.	
7. 7.16 —do—	Day spent in cleaning up.	
8. 7.16 —do—	Bn moved to TRIGGER WOOD	
9 pm 9. 7.16 TRIGGER WOOD	Bn moved to original British trench North of MARICOURT	
10. 7.16 TRONES WOOD	TRONES WOOD Operation. Casualties Major HIGGINS & 2 Lt T.M. SPROAT killed. 2 Lt R. MICHAELIS, M.J. CRAIG, D.M. RIDDELL, H. MEYER, D.W.R. BELLANY wounded killed OR M. wounded 79 missing 28. Draft 1/0 OR arrived from 7½ Bn.	Reference Appendix I
12.15 am 13. 3. 16 —do—	Bn relieved by 6.7 Bn West Kents & moved to TRIGGER WOOD	
8 am 13. 7.16 TRIGGER WOOD	Bn moved to BOIS DES TAILLES	
14. 7.16 BOIS DES TAILLES	Bn moved to CORBIE	

Army Form C. 2118.

WAR DIARY
or
INTELLIGENCE SUMMARY

(Erase heading not required.)

Instructions regarding War Diaries and Intelligence Summaries are contained in F. S. Regs., Part II. and the Staff Manual respectively. Title pages will be prepared in manuscript.

Hour, Date, Place	Summary of Events and Information	Remarks and references to Appendices
14.7.16 CORBIE	Bn in billets	
15.7.16 —do—	Parade/on GOC Division at VAUX-SUR-SOMME	
16.7.16 —do—	Draft 69 OR arrived	
17.7.16 —do—	15627 SGT WARD & 16013 CPL SHAINE awarded MILITARY MEDALS for acts of Bravery in TRONES WOOD.	
18.7.16 —do—	—do—	
19.7.16 —do—	—do—	
9am 20.7.16 HAPPY VALLEY	Bn moved to HAPPY VALLEY	
	Bn moved to Camp at pt 71 NORTH on BRAY-FRICOURT RD	
	MAJOR G. ROLLO appointed to command 13th Bn K.L.R.	
21.7.16 PT 71 NORTH	Quiet day in bivouacs	
22.7.16 —do—	—do— ready to move at ½ hr notice	
6 pm	Orders received that attack on GUILLEMONT was postponed	
23.7.16 —do—	In bivouacs	
24.7.16 —do—	Warned to be ready to move to attack GUILLEMONT, cancelled towards evening	
25.7.16 —do—	Special parade for GOC Division	
26.7.16 —do—	Bn in bivouacs. Draft of 45 OR arrived	

WAR DIARY
or
INTELLIGENCE SUMMARY
(Erase heading not required.)

Army Form C. 2118.

Hour, Date, Place	Summary of Events and Information	Remarks and references to Appendices
27.7.16 Pt 71 NORTH	Bn in Bivouac. Reinforcement 2nd Lt A.C. DOUGLASS A.P. WATSON W.H. PIERCE W.S. STANDRING J.F. GOODALL Awards D.S.O 2nd Lt (Temp Capt) H.W. BRINSON Military Cross 2 Lt J.M. SPROAT	
28.7.16	Bn in Bivouac. GOC 30th Div awarded Croix de Guerre to 23658 Pte BRASS 26116 Pte MILES (wounded) also awarded the medal	
9 pm 29.7.16	Bn moved up to assembly positions for attack in German system J trenches from GUILLEMONT exclusive to FALFEMONT FARM inclusive	
4.45 am 30.7.16	Zero hour. The Bn was in support to 19th & 2 Cos behind 20th Bn KLR. 2 Cos behind 19th & 2 Cos behind 2nd. Very thick mist. The attack was pushed home to the objective in places but in the main our line was held up by machine gun fire from hidden machine guns.	

WAR DIARY
or
INTELLIGENCE SUMMARY
(Erase heading not required.)

Army Form C. 2118.

Hour, Date, Place	Summary of Events and Information	Remarks and references to Appendices

	Fighting continued all day sweeping backwards & forwards but by 6pm about 300 yds in depth that been gained & consolidated all along our front. Counter...
	
	 Killed Officers 2-Lt ER PORRITT
	 " R.H. SMITH
	 " J.J. FARIS (att 20th LR)
	 " F.E. BOUNDY (att 89th TMB)
	
	 Died of wounds ACTING CAPT M.N. BRINSON
	 Wounded 27 2/Lt J. THOMPSON
	 " E.W. WILLMER
	 " J.R. BLABEY
	 2 " F.D. PEET
	 " G.M. MORRIS
	 " J.F.W. BERRY
	 " W.H. JOHNSTON
	 " T. LANGLEY
	 " E.T. LEWIS
	 " W.S. STANDRING
	
	 Killed OR 36
	 Wounded " 130
	 Missing " 95
	  ————
	  261	

WAR DIARY
or
INTELLIGENCE SUMMARY

(Erase heading not required.)

Army Form C. 2118.

Hour, Date, Place	Summary of Events and Information	Remarks and references to Appendices
3 am 31.7.16	Relief by 4th King's Own Duke of Lancaster's Regt commenced	
5 am 31.7.16	Relief complete & Bn returned to camp at Pt 71 NORTH	
	J Beck Capt. 17th Kings (Liverpool) Regt	

89th Inf Bde 30th Divn

1.

Notes by Lt. Colonel B.C. Fairfax

Commanding 17th Bn. The King's

on the fighting at TRONES WOOD 10th, 11th & 12th July 1916.

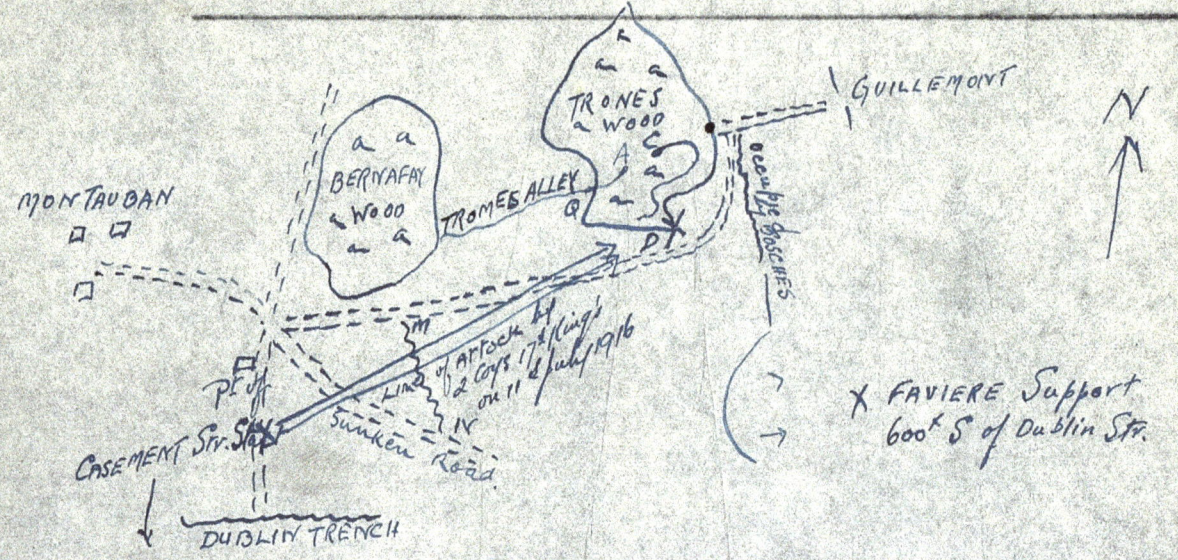

1. **Monday 10th July.** – 90th Infantry Bde. holding the right sector of the British front, and with an undefined footing in TRONES WOOD.

8 a.m. 1 Company 17th King's lent to 90th Infantry Bde.

9:30 P.M. This Company ordered to attack TRONES WOOD, and to relieve a portion of the 90th Bde. garrisoning it.

(The 89th Infantry Bde was to relieve 90th Infantry Bde. during night 10th/11th July).

(This attack was a failure, and the Company 17th King's suffered heavily).

10 p.m. Second Company 17th King's placed under orders of 90th Infantry Bde., and ordered by 90th Infantry Bde to reinforce 16th Manchesters in SUNKEN ROAD – subsequently this Company 17th King's was withdrawn by 89th Bde, to BRICQUETERIE ROAD.

2. Situation on the early morning 11th July as regards the British "hold" of TRONES WOOD appears to be that we had no "hold" of TRONES WOOD.

11th July. – During the day our "hold" of TRONES WOOD materialised under 89th Bde., but about 10p.m. was again not satisfactory.

Dispositions of 17th Bn. King's at 10 p.m.

1 Company in trench N.- W and SUNKEN ROAD.

1 Company (remnants of) in DUBLIN STREET.

2 Companies in DUBLIN & CASEMENTS STREETS.

Battn. H.Q. in PAVIERE SUPPORT.

5. At 10:15 p.m. I received orders to take my 2 Companies from DUBLIN and CASEMENT STREETS to TRONES WOOD, clear up the situation there, and remain there. No time was to be lost, as the situation was precarious. Time being of importance, I telephoned to my 2 Company Commanders (Capt. Brinson and Lieut Thompson) that I would meet them on the BRICQUETERIE Road at DUBLIN STREET in 10 minutes, and for them to have their Companies ready to move. The Companies were ready when I arrived, and I spent 5 minutes explaining briefly to the officers my intentions. I mention this to emphasize the intelligence and skill of Capt. Brinson and Lieut Thompson in carrying out my orders, (as I shall describe later), with so little preparations and explanation.

10:30 p.m. 2 Companies moved off from a slight cutting in the BRICQUETIE - MARICOURT ROAD, a short distance N. of DUBLIN STREET, straight for the S.E. corner of TRONES WOOD, the trees of which stood out against the sky.

The question of what is the best formation for troops to adopt whilst moving across a shell swept zone is always a moot one. My experiences leads me to the conviction that "petits pacquets" are the best, especially by night.

I, myself, with a special party of 6 scouts, walked straight to the S.E. corner of TRONES WOOD, somewhat in advance of and on the right flank of the 2 Companies.

Within about 200^x of that point, I collected my party in a shell hole and explained what I wanted, namely to slip quietly into the wood and look out for Machine Guns. This they did, bumped into a Machine Gun, and four of them were killed or wounded, I went into the wood and met my Company Commanders, who had also succeeded in entering the wood and lining up their men on the alignment shewn on the sketch D-C. We all got busy digging and by 4 a.m. next morning were down six foot. A small attack was made on us about 1 a.m. from the east, which failed.

I should like again to praise my Officers for their great skill and bravery in personnelly tracing the trench line, it afforded good protection from the East, S-E, and North. Capt. Brinson went twice to get in touch with the 20th King's to the south, but on each occasion was fired on by Germans and the 20th King's.

I should have stated that I met the seniour Officer of the two Companies of the second Battn. Bedfordshire Regt. about midnight on the 11/12th in my hole in TRONES WOOD. This Officer explained his positions to me, which were as shown on sketch, viz:- a wedge of about 80^x from A to Q into TRONES WOOD, the remainder of his men being in TRONES ALLEY. <u>This was the only British "hold" on TRONES WOOD at about 11:30 p.m. on the night of 11th July-when the 2 Coys 17th King's took up the line D to C.</u> Whilst getting on to this line D to C, my 2 Companies encountered no organised opposition, though dug-outs were entered and a few Germans killed. The essence of my original instructions was "not to attempt too Much" but "make sure what we did get". These instructions were admirably carried out.

4. At dawn on 12th July the situation was very satisfactory and but for a very intence artillery bombardment I felt there was no chance of our being ousted. As a matter of fact, men had to be withdrawn Northwards temporarly from the southern piece of trench owing to heavy shelling there, or at least thinned out. At about 7:30 a.m. I went Bde. H.Q. at the BRICQUETERIE. Plans were then made to further strengthen the 89th Bde. hold on TRONES WOOD, and it was decided:-

<u>12th July. 1 p.m.</u>

1. Join up C to A - I, E, the Bedford wedge and 17th trench
2. Wire the whole front Q.A.C.D. at 1 p.m. I met the Officer of the 2nd Battn Bedfords and my own at point P, having

been appointed O.C. TRONES WOOD. Small covering parties were put out, and digging and wireing put in hand by parties of 2nd Bedfords and 17th King's. There was a considerable amount of sniping from the very dense woods in front, but the covering parties were so well handled that I do not think the Germans had an idea what was being done.

12th July 6 p.m. Wiring and digging complete all day an intermittent bombardment was kept up on the south part of TRONES WOOD and our heavy guns "arrosed" the centre and north of the wood, paying particular attention to the strong point on the eastern edge, where the GUILLEMONT Road strikes the wood

5. Twice during the night of the 12th the Germans made half hearted attacks on our line Q.A.C., and southwards, and appeared surprised to find wire and organized opposition. On one occasion a party got hung up in the wire/disposed of and were by a Lewis Gun.

About midnight 12th July. 1 Company 4th R.West Kents relieved 2 Companies of 17th King's, and 1 Company ditto, the 2 Coys (both considerably reduced) 2nd Battn Bedfordshire Regt. I myself reported personally at the BRICQUETERIE to 89th Bde. H.Q. and my Companies moved to TRIGGER WOOD about dawn. The 2 Companies of my own Battalion and still more so, the 2 Companies 2nd Bedfordshires had had a rough time.
The Officers and men behaved magnificently.

Conclusive.

1. Leadership is the difficulty, and control.
2. I am strongly in favour of movement by sections in file. By night, more particularly, there appears to me but slight hope of direction being maintained and objectives reached by troops moving in any other formation than file or single file.
3. I attribute the successful entry of my 2 Companies on the night of 11th July to the adoption of this method of moving, and to the skill of the individual leaders.

3.

BRIQUETERIE - HARICOURT ROAD, a short distance N. of DUBLIN
STREET, straight for the S.E. corner of TRONES WOOD, the trees
of which stood out against the sky.
The question of what is the best formation for troops to adopt
whilst moving across a shell swept zone is always a moot one.
My experience leads me to the conviction that "petits paquets"
are the best, especially at by night.
I, myself, with a special party of six scouts, walked straight
to the S.E. corner of TRONES WOOD, somewhat in advance of and on
the right flank of the 2 companies. Within about 800" of that
point, I collected my party in a shell hole and explained what
I wanted, namely to slip quietly into the wood and look out for
machine guns. This they did, bumped into a machine gun, and
four of them were killed or wounded. I went into the wood and
met my company commanders, who had also succeeded in entering the
wood and lining up their men on the alignment shown on the sketch
D-C. We all got busy digging, and by 4 a.m. next morning were
down 6 feet. A small attack was made on us about 4 a.m. from
the East, which failed.

I should like again to praise my officers for their
great skill and bravery in personally tracing the trench line.
It afforded good protection from the East, S.East, and North.
Captain BRINGON went twice to get in touch with the 20th King's
to the South, but on each occasion was fired on by Germans and
the 20th King's.

I should have stated that I met the senior
officer of the 2 companies of the 2nd Battn. Bedfordshire Regiment
about midnight on 14th/15th in my hole in TRONES WOOD. This
officer explained his dispositions to me, which were as shown on
sketch, viz:- a wedge of about 30" from A to C into TRONES WOOD,
the remainder of his men being in TRONES ALLEY. This was the
only British "hold" on TRONES WOOD at about 11.30 p.m. on the
night of 14th July - when the 2 companies 17th King's took up
the line D to C. Whilst getting on to this line D to C, my
2 companies encountered no organised opposition, though dug outs
were entered and a few Germans killed.
The essence of my original instructions was "not to attempt too
much" but to "make sure of what we did get". These
instructions were admirably carried out.

4. At dawn on 15th July the situation was very satisfactory, and
but for a very intense artillery bombardment I felt there was no
chance of our being ousted. As a matter of fact, men had to be
withdrawn Northwards temporarily from the southern piece of
trench owing to heavy shelling there, or at least thinned out.
At about 7.30 a.m. I went to Bde. H.Q. at the BRIQUETERIE.
Plans were then made to further strengthen the 20th Bde. hold
on TRONES WOOD, and it was decided:-
15th July. 4 p.m.
A. Join up C to A - i.e. the Bedford wedge and 17th Trench.
C. Wire the whole front B.A.C.D. At 1 p.m. I met the officer
of the 2nd Battn. Bedfords and my own at Point F, having been
appointed O.C. TRONES WOOD. Small covering parties were put
out, and digging and wiring put in hand by parties of 2nd
Bedfords and 17th King's. There was a considerable amount of
sniping from the very dense woods in front, but the covering
parties were so well handled that I do not think the Germans
had an idea what was being done.
15th July. 4 a.m. Wiring and digging complete.

All day an intermittent bombardment was kept up on the S. part
of TRONES WOOD, and our own heavy guns "arrosed" the centre and
North of the wood, paying particular attention to the strong
point on the Eastern edge, where the GUILLEMONT Road strikes the
wood.

5. Twice during the night of the 15th the Germans made half hearted

attacks on our line Q & C and southwards, and appeared surprised to find wire and organised opposition. On one occasion a party got hung up in the wire, and were disposed of by a Lewis Gun.

About midnight 13th July. A company 4th R. West Kents relieved 2 companies of 17th King's, and 1 company ditto. the 2 companies (both considerably reduced) 2nd Battn. Bedfordshire Regt. I myself reported personally at the BRIQUETERIE to 76th Bde. H.Q., and my companies moved to TRIGGER WOOD about dawn. The 2 companies of my own Battalion and, still more so, the 2 companies 2nd Bedfordshires had had a rough time.
The officers and men behaved magnificently.

CONCLUSIONS.

1. Leadership is the difficulty, and control.

2. I am strongly in favour of movement by sections in file. By night, more particularly, there appears to me but slight hope of direction being maintained and objectives reached by troops moving in any other formation than file or single file.

3. I attribute the successful entry of my 2 companies on the night of 11th July to the adoption of this method of moving, and to the skill of the individual leaders.

4. Men must be lightly equipped to fight, particularly in wood fighting.

5. It is no use soldiers wandering through woods and saying they have taken them - it only leads to annihilation. A firm footing - i.e. a trench 6' deep and wire in front must be made and put up first on some definite alignment. From this trench further progress can be made by specially chosen parties. An advance in a wood must be deliberate and cunning. Heroic action probably ends in disaster.

6. A wood, such as TRONES WOOD, should be treated with respect, and slow progress for its occupation expected only.

7. Proximity to German Infantry in a wood should be a satisfactory position for British Infantry to be in, as they are unlikely to be shelled by German guns.

89th Brigade.
30th Division.

1/17th BATTALION

THE KING'S LIVERPOOL REGIMENT

AUGUST 1916

Army Form C. 2118.

WAR DIARY
or
INTELLIGENCE SUMMARY

(Erase heading not required.)

Instructions regarding War Diaries and Intelligence Summaries are contained in F. S. Regs., Part II. and the Staff Manual respectively. Title pages will be prepared in manuscript.

Hour, Date, Place		Summary of Events and Information	Remarks and references to Appendices
	CITADEL Camp PT 71 NORTH		
	1.8.16	Bn in Bivouac	
4.15 am	2.8.16	Bn left Camp, 27 OR B.C. FAIRFAX evacuated sick	
8 am	—	Bn entrained for LONGPRES	
3 pm	DERNANCOURT	Bn detrained & marched to DOUDELAINVILLE	
	LONGPRES		
9 pm	DOUDELAINVILLE	Bn arrived in billets	
7.00 pm	3.8.16	Bn left & marched to PONT REMY	
11 pm	PONT REMY	Bn entrained for MERVILLE	
8 am	4.8.16 MERVILLE	Bn arrived detrained & marched to CALONNE	
10.30 am	CALONNE	Bn in billets. Reinforcements 6 OR & 396 OR	
	5.8.16	(6=7=8=9= & 10= KLR)	
	—	Bn in billets - Reinforcements 47 OR (6= KLR)	
	6.8.16	9 OR (frm 20= KLR)	
	7.8.16	48 OR attached to 19= KLR	
	8.8.16	bn retained in strength of the Bn	
	9.8.16	Bn in billets - reinforcements 38 OR (15, 13 & 19= KLR)	
4.30 pm	10.8.16	Bn left CALONNE for LES LOBES.	
	—	100 OR posted to the Bn sent for attachment to 19= KLR	
4.5	—	20= KLR	

WAR DIARY or INTELLIGENCE SUMMARY

Army Form C. 2118.

(Erase heading not required.)

Instructions regarding War Diaries and Intelligence Summaries are contained in F. S. Regs., Part II. and the Staff Manual respectively. Title pages will be prepared in manuscript.

Hour, Date, Place			Summary of Events and Information	Remarks and references to Appendices
6.30pm	10.8.16	LES LOBES	Bn arrived in billets.	
	11.8.16	—	Bn in billets – Bombing team firing, Snipers training the Coy squad drill	
	12.8.16	—	Bn in billets – specialists training as above	
	13.8.16	—		
			Reinforcements 2/Lt N. B. FEARN ⎫	
			" W. G. BILLINGTON ⎬ from	
			" H. E. A. PULMAN ⎪ 18th K.L.R	
			" N. SMITH ⎪	
			" C. B. ARNOLD ⎪	
			" A. S. BOSTON ⎭	
	14.8.16	—	Bn in billets – specialist training continued & Route march	
			Reinforcements Lt I.V.H. CAMPBELL (12th Kings)	
			F/Lt K.G. COLLIN ⎫	
			" L.N. WINZER ⎬	
			" S.G. RICE (1/28 London Regt)	
			" N. HENRY (1/6 K.L.R)	
			" J.R. WHITE (1/6 K.L.R)	
	15.8.16	—	" training continued	
	16.8.16	—	Bn in billets " " "	

Army Form C. 2118.

WAR DIARY
or
INTELLIGENCE SUMMARY
(Erase heading not required.)

Instructions regarding War Diaries and Intelligence Summaries are contained in F.S. Regs., Part II. and the Staff Manual respectively. Title pages will be prepared in manuscript.

Hour, Date, Place		Summary of Events and Information	Remarks and references to Appendices
18.8.16. 10 am	LES LOBES	Bn left for HINGETTE	
18.8.16 11 am	HINGETTE	Bn arrived HINGETTE	
19.8.16 to 23.8.16	—	Bn in billets, training continued	
24.8.16 3 pm	LA PANNERIE	The Bn was on duty for presentation of ribbons (honors & awards) to 30th, 31st & 61st Divisions by 1st Army Commander - General Sir HAKING. Bn formed up 3 sides of a square with regiment in centre. After general salute the ribbons were pinned & finally the Bn marched past the recipients of awards. Brigade sports. Bn was successful in	
25.8.16	—	100 yds - En. Sgt maj LOVELADY ¼ mile cross country } PTE OLLEY 1 mile Team swimming race Boxing 8.6 & under - PTE CARGILL Football - 6 a side (2nd LT ARNOLD Capt.)	

Army Form C. 2118.

WAR DIARY
or
INTELLIGENCE SUMMARY
(Erase heading not required.)

Instructions regarding War Diaries and Intelligence Summaries are contained in F. S. Regs., Part II. and the Staff Manual respectively. Title pages will be prepared in manuscript.

Hour, Date, Place	Summary of Events and Information	Remarks and references to Appendices
26/8/16 HINGETTE	Bn in billets – Reinforcement Capt Horser (15"Kings)	
27.8.16 5pm	Bn left HINGETTE	
27.8.16 7pm GORRE	Bn arrived in billets at GORRE	
28.8.16	—	
29.8.16	Working parties for RE supplied daily.	
30.8.16	Bn left GORRE to relieve 19th Bn K.L.R in Right Subsector of GIVENCHY sector	
31.8.16 5pm		
8.15pm GIVENCHY SECTOR	Relief Complete.	

J. W. Beck. Major.
Commanding 17th Bn King's (Liverpool) Regt

vol 11

11.C.
5 sheets

— CONFIDENTIAL —

WAR DIARY.

OF

17TH BN. KING'S LIVERPOOL REGT.

FROM: 1ST SEPTEMBER 1916.   TO: 30TH SEPTEMBER 1916.

(VOLUME XI.)

Army Form C. 2118.

WAR DIARY
or
INTELLIGENCE SUMMARY

(Erase heading not required.)

Instructions regarding War Diaries and Intelligence Summaries are contained in F. S. Regs., Part II. and the Staff Manual respectively. Title pages will be prepared in manuscript.

[Stamp: 17TH (SERVICE) BATT. ORDERLY ROOM - 2 OCT. 1916 THE LIVERPOOL REGT.]

Hour, Date, Place	Summary of Events and Information	Remarks and references to Appendices
1. 9. 16 GIVENCHY LEFT SUBSECTOR	Bn in the line	
2. 9. 16		
3. 9. 16		
4. 9. 16 4 pm	19th started to relieve us.	
8 pm	Relief complete.	
8 pm	Bn in support in village line.	
5. 9. 16 VILLAGE LINE		
6. 9. 16		
7. 9. 16		
8. 9. 16 5 pm	2nd in Wilts commenced to relieve us.	
8. 9. 16 8 pm	Relief complete.	
8. 9. 16 10 pm BETHUNE	Bn arrive in billets at BETHUNE.	
9. 9. 16		
10. 9. 16		
11. 9. 16	Bn in billets at BETHUNE.	
12. 9. 16		
13. 9. 16		

WAR DIARY or INTELLIGENCE SUMMARY

Army Form C. 2118.

(Erase heading not required.)

Hour, Date, Place			Summary of Events and Information	Remarks and references to Appendices
14.9.16	10.24 am	BETHUNE	Bn left BETHUNE by train for SAVY.	Ry LENS 1/100,000
14.9.16	2.45 pm	SAVY	Bn detrained at SAVY	
14.9.16	6 pm	ÉCOIVRES	Bn arrived at ÉCOIVRES (XVII Corps - 60 Div - 180 Bde)	
15.9.16	5 pm		A & B Coys left for dugouts in forward area at MAISON BLANCHE & MOISSONEUSE for work under 180 Bde	
16.9.16	1.30 am		Orders received to be ready to move at 8 am	
—	7 am		A & B Coys arrived back	
—	8 am		Bn ready to move - orders received later that move was postponed till following morning	
15.9.16		Reinforcements	Reinforcements 30 OR Ranks joined. 2nd Lt LAPULMAN & LT REMINDER to F.A. Dienan.	
16.9.16				
17.9.16	9 am		Bn left ÉCOIVRES	
17.9.16	11.20 am	VILLERS CHATEL	Bn arrived in billets - orders received that Bn would entrain at SAVY at 12.38 pm 19 inst - destination unknown	
18.9.16			Bn in billets - baths at AUBIGNY (XVII Corps)	

Army Form C. 2118.

WAR DIARY
or
INTELLIGENCE SUMMARY

(Erase heading not required.)

Instructions regarding War Diaries and Intelligence Summaries are contained in F.S. Regs., Part II. and the Staff Manual respectively. Title pages will be prepared in manuscript.

Hour, Date, Place		Summary of Events and Information	Remarks and references to Appendices
19.9.16	10.45 a.m.	Batn. marched from VILLERS CHATEL, entraining at SAVY BERLETTE at 11.30 a.m.	
	3.45 p.m. 5.30 p.m.	Detrained at DOULLENS. marched to GEZAINCOURT, arriving at 5.30 p.m.	
20.9.16 GEZAINCOURT		Bn. in Billets at GEZAINCOURT.	
21.9.16	7.30 a.m. 12 noon.	Bn. marched at 7.30 a.m. from GEZAINCOURT to VIGNACOURT, arriving at 12 noon.	
22.9.16 VIGNACOURT		2nd Lt. D.P. Cross attached from 4th Bn. Bedfordshire Regt. as acting Adjutant. Capt. R.G. Beazley (Adjutant) attached to H.Q. 30th Divn. as Camp Commandant.	
23.9.16 24.9.16 25.9.16 26.9.16 27.9.16 28.9.16 29.9.16 30.9.16	VIGNACOURT — do —	In billets. Intensive Training.	

[signature]
LIEUT COLONEL
COMDG 17th (SERVICE) BATT: THE LIVERPOOL REGT

Army Form C. 2118.

WAR DIARY
or
INTELLIGENCE SUMMARY

(Erase heading not required.)

Instructions regarding War Diaries and Intelligence Summaries are contained in F.S. Regs., Part II. and the Staff Manual respectively. Title pages will be prepared in manuscript.

Hour, Date, Place	Summary of Events and Information	Remarks and references to Appendices
1-10-16. VIGNACOURT.	Battalion in Billets. Intensive Training.	
2-10-16. - do -	Battalion in Billets. Intensive Training.	
3-10-16. - do -	Battalion in Billets.	
11.30 a.m. 4.10.16.	Battalion left VIGNACOURT in Motor Buses.	
2.15 P.M. - " -	Arrived at RIBEMONT, and marched to DERNANCOURT,	
5.30 P.M. - " -	arriving in Billets at 5.30 P.M.	
5-10-16. DERNANCOURT.	Battalion in Billets.	
6-10-16. - do -	Battalion in Billets. Ordinary Training, Arm Drill, Bayonet Fighting etc., by Companies.	
7-10-16. - do -	Battalion in Billets. Ordinary Training by Companies. Village Attack Practice in morning.	
8-10-16. - do -	Battalion in Billets. Village Attack Practice in morning.	
4 P.M. - " -	Brigade Parade for Speech by G.O.C., Division.	
9-10-16. - do -	Battalion in Billets. Village Attack Practice.	
7 A.M. 10-10-16.	Battalion marched from DERNANCOURT under Bde.O.O.58 to S.21.b, and rested at this point for dinner and tea. Transport and Quartermaster's Stores moved to X.30.a.5/5.	
5 P.M. - " -	Battalion moved off in file to relieve a Battalion of 123rd Infantry Brigade in Front Line N.W. of FLERS, via LONGUEVAL, and across country.	
6.30 A.M. 11-10-16.	Relief completed.	

WAR DIARY
or
INTELLIGENCE SUMMARY

(Erase heading not required.)

Army Form C. 2118.

Hour, Date, Place	Summary of Events and Information	Remarks and references to Appendices
11-10-16. GIRD TRENCH AND GIRD SUPPORT.	Battalion in Front Line and Support Trenches. British bombardment of enemy Front Line System commenced about midday. Hostile shelling was intermittent throughout the day. CASUALTIES:- 2nd Lt. N. SMITH and 2nd Lt. J.H. FEARON wounded. 7 O.R. Killed and 22 O.R. wounded.	
12-10-16. -do- 2.5 P.M.	Our Bombardment continued. Enemy reply weak. Zero hour. Attack on Burnam Front Line System commenced. Enemy wire was found to be uncut, and attack was unsuccessful. Hostile Machine Gun fire was very heavy, and caused many casualties. Battalion H.Q. and Support Trench were heavily shelled throughout afternoon and evening. Small Section of 20th Battn. K.L.R. (in Support) only succeeded in reaching our Front Line at about 5 P.M., after which hour the Supports gradually got into position. During this action, all communication had to be carried out by Runners and Carrier Pigeons, as all wires were being continually cut by enemy shelling. CASUALTIES:- Killed - Capt. S.C.S. HORSER, 2nd Lt. K.G. COLLIN	
5 P.M. -"-		

WAR DIARY or INTELLIGENCE SUMMARY

Army Form C. 2118.

Hour, Date, Place	Summary of Events and Information	Remarks and references to Appendices
12-10-16. GIRD TRENCH. AND GIRD SUPPORT.	CASUALTIES – Killed (contd). 2nd Lt. S. J. IRELAND, 2nd Lt. W. HORNBY, 2nd Lt. J. G. DIXON. Wounded :- Lieut. I. V. H. CAMPBELL, 2nd Lt. A. P. WATSON, 2nd Lt. A. S. BOSTON, 2nd Lt. J. R. WHITTLE, 2nd Lt. F. H. THRAVES. Killed – 38 O.R. Wounded Missing etc. about 225 O.R.	
13-10-16. – do –	19th Battn. K.L.R. came into position in Support Lines during the early morning.	
9 A.M. – " –	Battalion relieved by Companies of 19th + 20th Battn. K.L.R., and moved off to FLERS SUPPORT.	
2 P.M. – " –	Battalion relieved in FLERS SUPPORT by 19th Bn. Manchester Regt., and moved out of Line to	
5.30 P.M. – " – . S.26. Central.	Bivouacs at S.26. Central, arriving at 5.30 P.M. 2nd Lt. A. P. WATSON Died of Wounds. Battalion in bivouacs.	
14-10-16. S.26. Central.	– do –	
15-10-16. – do –	– " –	
16-10-16. – do –	– do –	
17-10-16. – do –	– do –	
3.30 A.M. 18-10-16. – do –	Reinforcement of 48 O.R. arrived from 24th I.B.D.	
7 A.M. – " –	Received orders from Brigade to be prepared to move off at one hour's notice. Battalion standing by for remainder of day.	

WAR DIARY
or
INTELLIGENCE SUMMARY

(Erase heading not required.)

Army Form C. 2118.

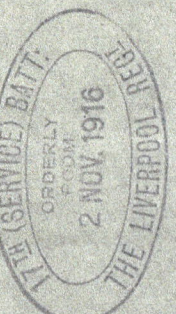

Hour, Date, Place	Summary of Events and Information	Remarks and references to Appendices
19-10-16. S.26. Central.	Battalion in Bivouacs.	
8 A.M. 20-10-16.	Battalion moved off to Brigade Reserve in CREST TRENCH, relieving 19th Battn. K.L.R.	
21-10-16. CREST TRENCH.	Battalion in Reserve Trenches.	
22-10-16. - do -	- do -	
3 P.M. - " -	Relieved by Battalion of 5th Australian Division and marched back to Rear Area at MAMETZ WOOD CAMP, arriving in Bivouacs at 6 P.M.	
6 P.M. - " - MAMETZ WOOD CAMP.	Reinforcement of 145 O.R. arrived.	
23-10-16. - do -	Battalion in Bivouacs.	
8 A.M. 24-10-16.	Battalion marched from MAMETZ WOOD CAMP at 8 A.M. to BUIRE-SOUS-CORBIE, arriving in camp at 2 P.M.	
2 P.M. - " - BUIRE-SOUS-CORBIE.		
25-10-16. - do -	Battalion in Camp.	
11 A.M. 26-10-16.	Battalion marched from BUIRE-SOUS-CORBIE and entrained at EDGE HILL RAILHEAD at 12 noon.	
12 noon - " -	Detrained at DOULLENS, and marched to HALLOY.	
10 P.M. - " -		
2.30 A.M. 27-10-16. HALLOY.	Arrived at HALLOY. Arrived in Huts, men in Huts, men in Huts.	

WAR DIARY or INTELLIGENCE SUMMARY

Army Form C. 2118.

Hour, Date, Place	Summary of Events and Information	Remarks and references to Appendices
1.55 P.M. 28-10-16. POMMIER.	Battalion marched from HALLOY to Billets in POMMIER, arriving at 6 P.M.	
6 P.M. -"-		
2 P.M. 29-10-16. -do-	Battalion marched from POMMIER to Front Line (Right Sub-Section), and relieved 5th Battn. Leicestershire Regt. Battn. in Front Line Trenches.	
30-10-16.	REINFORCEMENT:- 2nd Lts. C. BASINGHAM, G.A. CRAWFORD, C.L. CHILDS, D.C.H. FRASER, B.S. DAVIS. Battn. in Front Line Trenches.	
31-10-16.	REINFORCEMENT:- 2nd Lt. G.H.C. TRUSCOTT.	

[Stamp: 17th (SERVICE) BATT. ORDERLY ROOM 2 NOV 1916 THE LIVERPOOL REGT.]

_____ LIEUT. COLONEL
COMdg 17th (SERVICE) BATT. THE LIVERPOOL REGT.

Vol 13

13.C.
5 sheets

CONFIDENTIAL.

WAR DIARY

OF

17TH BATTN KINGS (LIVERPOOL) REGIMENT.

From 1st November 1916.   To 30th November 1916

VOLUME 13.

Army Form C. 2118

WAR DIARY
or
INTELLIGENCE SUMMARY
(Erase heading not required.)

Instructions regarding War Diaries and Intelligence Summaries are contained in F. S. Regs., Part II. and the Staff Manual respectively. Title Pages will be prepared in manuscript.

Place	Date	Hour	Summary of Events and Information	Remarks and references to Appendices
	1/11/16		Battn. in Front line Trenches. CASUALTY: 1 o.r. Wounded.	
	2/11/16		- do -	
	3/11/16		- do -	
	4/11/16	4 P.M.	Battn. relieved in Front line Trenches by 19th Battn. K.L.R. and moved into Billets in BIENVILLERS. (Support).	
BIENVILLERS	5/11/16		Battn. engaged on Working Parties under R.E. during day.	
- do -	6/11/16		- do -	
			CASUALTY: 1 o.r. Killed. REINFORCEMENT: 2nd Lt. W.B. HOLME arrived.	
- do -	7/11/16		Battn. engaged on Working Parties under R.E. during day.	
- do -	8/11/16		- do -	
- do -	9/11/16		- do -	
			REINFORCEMENT: 5 o.r.	
	10/11/16	4.15 P.M.	Battn. relieved 19th Battn. K.L.R. in Right Subsector. CASUALTIES: 5 o.r. Wounded.	
	11/11/16		Battn. in Front line Trenches. CASUALTY: Wounded 1 o.r.	
	12/11/16		Battn. in Front line Trenches. CASUALTIES: 1 o.r. Killed. 5 o.r. Wounded.	
	13/11/16		Battn. in Front line Trenches.	
	14/11/16		Battn. in Front line Trenches.	
	15/11/16		Battn. in Front line Trenches.	
	16/11/16	3. P.M.	Battn. relieved by 19th Battn. K.L.R. & moved into Rest Billets	

Army Form C. 2118

WAR DIARY
or
INTELLIGENCE SUMMARY
(Erase heading not required.)

Instructions regarding War Diaries and Intelligence Summaries are contained in F. S. Regs., Part II. and the Staff Manual respectively. Title Pages will be prepared in manuscript.

Place	Date	Hour	Summary of Events and Information	Remarks and references to Appendices
POMMIER	16/11/16		at POMMIER (Divisional Reserve). Arrived in Billets.	
— " —	17/11/16	6.PM	Battn. in Billets. POMMIER.	
— " —	18/11/16	10 A.M.	Battn. marched from POMMIER to Hutments at HUMBERCAMPS.	
HUMBERCAMPS	— " —	11 A.M.	Arrived in Huts.	
— " —	19/11/16	2.PM	Battn. moved from Hutments into Billets in the Village.	
— " —	20/11/16		In Billets. Training:- Bombing, Arm + Squad Drill.	
— " —	21/1/16		— do —	
— " —	22/11/16		— do —	
— " —	— " —	12 noon	Battn. marched from HUMBERCAMPS to Front Line Trenches, and relieved 19th Battn. K.L.R.	
— " —	— " —	4.10.PM.	Relief complete.	
— " —	23/11/16		Battn. in Front Line Trenches. REINFORCEMENT. 1 O.R.	
— " —	24/11/16		— do — REINFORCEMENT. 2 O.R.	
— " —	25/11/16		— do — Capt. R.O. WYNNE attached from 2nd Bn. Bedfordshire Regiment to assume Temporary Command, vice Lt. Col. J.N. PECK, Proceeding on Course.	
— " —	26/11/16		Lt. Col. J.N. PECK Proceeded for Course at Third Army Infantry School. In Front line Trenches.	
— " —	27/11/16		— do —	
— " —	— " —		CASUALTY. 1 O.R. Killed.	

Army Form C. 2118

WAR DIARY
or
INTELLIGENCE SUMMARY
(Erase heading not required.)

Instructions regarding War Diaries and Intelligence Summaries are contained in F.S. Regs., Part II. and the Staff Manual respectively. Title Pages will be prepared in manuscript.

Place	Date	Hour	Summary of Events and Information	Remarks and references to Appendices
BERLES.	25/11/16	3 P.M.	Battn. relieved by 19th Battn. K.L.R. & moved into Billets in BERLES (in Support).	
	29/11/16		Battn. in Support in BERLES. Engaged in Working Parties under R.E. during day.	
-,,-	30/11/16		Battn. in Support in BERLES. Working Parties etc.	

R.O. Wynne. Captain
~~Lieut Colonel~~
Comdg 17th (SERVICE) BATT: THE LIVERPOOL REGT

17TH (SERVICE) BATT:
ORDERLY ROOM
3 DEC. 1916
THE LIVERPOOL REGT

14.C.
6 sheets

Vol 14

CONFIDENTIAL.

WAR DIARY.

OF

17TH. BATTALION KING'S LIVERPOOL REGIMENT.

FROM 1ST DECEMBER 1916. TO 31ST DECEMBER 1916.

VOLUME 14.

Army Form C. 2118

WAR DIARY
or
INTELLIGENCE SUMMARY
(Erase heading not required.)

Instructions regarding War Diaries and Intelligence Summaries are contained in F. S. Regs., Part II. and the Staff Manual respectively. Title Pages will be prepared in manuscript.

Place	Date	Hour	Summary of Events and Information	Remarks and references to Appendices
BERLES.	1/12/16	-	Battalion in Support. Working Parties &c.	
- do -	2/12/16	-	- do -	
- do -	3/12/16	-	- do -	
	4/12/16	3.15 p.m.	Battalion relieved 19th Bn. K.L.R. in Front line Trenches (B.2. Subsector) Lt. Col. J.N PECK from Third Army School, resumed command.	
	5/12/16	-	Battalion in Front line Trenches. Capt. R.O. WYNNE returned to 2nd Bn. Bedford Regiment.	
	6/12/16	-	Battalion in Front line Trenches. Lieut (A/Capt) S.H. CHAPIN D.S.O. (Dragoon Guards) reported for duty.	
	7/12/16	-	Battalion in Front line Trenches.	
	8/12/16	-	- do -	
	9/12/16	-	- do -	
	10/12/16	-	- do - — CASUALTIES: 1 O.R. Killed. 3 O.R. Wounded.	
	- " -	3 p.m.	Battn. relieved by 19th Bn. K.L.R. & marched to Billets in	
	- " -	5.30 p.m.	HUMBERCAMPS. (1 Company in Huts). Major E.R.A. HALL reported for duty.	
HUMBERCAMPS.	11/12/16	-	Battalion in Billets Training:- Arms + Squad Drill.	
- do -	12/12/16	-	- do -	
- do -	13/12/16	-	- do -	
- do -	14/12/16	-	- do -	
- do -	15/12/16	-	- do -	

WAR DIARY or INTELLIGENCE SUMMARY

Army Form C. 2118

Instructions regarding War Diaries and Intelligence Summaries are contained in F. S. Regs., Part II. and the Staff Manual respectively. Title Pages will be prepared in manuscript.

(Erase heading not required.)

Place	Date	Hour	Summary of Events and Information	Remarks and references to Appendices
Reference Map. RANSART. 51.c. S.E. 3 + 4 (General) Edition 3.C. 1/10.000.	16/12/16 17/12/16	3 P.M.	Battalion relieved 19th Battn. K.L.R. in Front Line Trenches. (B.2. Subsector). Battn. in Front Line Trenches.	
		8 P.M.	PATROL. 2nd Lt. B.S. DAVIS with 1 N.C.O. + 4 men left Sap. 16.b. at 8 P.M. After proceeding due East he encountered enemy wire about 200 yards from the N.C.O./L/Cpl. FOSTER trench at Wi 25.b.80.40. — wires in except two middle Trenches + search party found entry life and Lt. DAVIS penetrated the German wire. Pre south end, being disturbed a fire, sleeps, viewed ammunition and [illegible] tripped on the middle wire line and exchanged bombs at about 15 ft. Pt. on L/Cpl. Foster [illegible] saw some German [illegible] patrol reaching Sap. 16.b. at about 11 P.M. Battalions in Front Line Trenches.	
	18/12/16	11 P.M.	—	
	19/12/16		do —	
	20/12/16		do —	
	21/12/16		do —	
Reference Map. RANSART. 51.c. S.E. 3 + 4 (General) Edition 3.C. 1/10.000.		5 P.M.	2nd Lieut. C.B. ARNOLD 1/c of Patrol of 2 N.C.O's + 10 men (with 1 Lewis gun), left our line at the Sunken Road Wi.15.c.2/9. Their object was to go along the Ravine to Wi.15.b.0/6. — When across to ROSE BANK, Wi.15.b.9/6 where they would lie in wait for any German Patrols. This being an approaching raid route. The L. Gun was to be placed at Wi.15.a.95/35. The Ravine was reached twice but the Patrol ran into a German Standing Patrol about Wi.15.b.1.5. The German Patrol opened heavy M. Gun + Rifle fire and three bombs at a range of about 8 yards. 2nd Lt. ARNOLD was wounded + 4 men hit and our Patrol retired. 2nd Lt. ARNOLD took shelter in a shell hole + one Private (Pte. EVANS), who advanced to reconnoitre the damage done and obtained M.G. fire to enable Pte. EVANS approached bodies lying on old ground + found that one man was apparently dead. Another ground	

WAR DIARY
or
INTELLIGENCE SUMMARY
(Erase heading not required.)

Army Form C. 2118

Place	Date	Hour	Summary of Events and Information	Remarks and references to Appendices
BERLES.	21/12/16.		Pte EVANS was unable to move him, and had to retire. The Lewis Gun was unable to fire during this encounter; as friend could not be distinguished from enemy. The N.C.O + 2 men with the L. Gun stayed out until ordered to come in at about 8.30 P.M. The enemy continued to send Very Lights into the Ravine constantly. TOTAL CASUALTIES:- 2nd Lt. C.B. ARNOLD and 1 O.R. wounded. 3 O.R. Missing (did not return).	
- do -	22/12/16	3 PM.	Battalion relieved in Front Line Trenches by 19th Battn. K.L.R., and moved into billets at BERLES (in Support).	
- do -	23/12/16		Battalion in Support. Working Parties etc.	
- do -	24/12/16		- do -	
- do -	- " -		- do -	
- do -	- " -	11.15 AM	Lt. Col. J.N. PECK proceeded on leave to England. Lieut (A/Capt). S.H. CHAPIN. D.S.O. assumed command of Battn.	
- do -	25/12/16		Enemy shelled Village with about 500 shells, ranging in calibre from 4.2" to 8". Christmas Day. - No Working Parties. Battalion in Support. Authority given for Lieut. S.H. CHAPIN. D.S.O. to wear the badges of the rank of Major, pending notification in "London Gazette".	
- do -	26/12/16.		Battalion in Support. - Working Parties. Enemy shelled Village intermittently until about 1.15 P.M., which 8", 5.9" and 4.2" shells. The Church received 4 direct hits, while the remainder fell within a radius of 100 yards. CASUALTY. 1 O.R. wounded in Working Party in the Trenches. (Rifle Reeves).	
- do -	27/12/16	11.15 AM	Battalion in Support moved to Battn. in Support posted to Battn. in effect from 25.12.16.	

WAR DIARY
or
INTELLIGENCE SUMMARY

(Erase heading not required.)

Army Form C. 2118

Place	Date	Hour	Summary of Events and Information	Remarks and references to Appendices
	28/12/16	3.20 P.M	Battn. relieved 19th Battn. K.L.R. in Front line Trenches. (B.2 Subsector)	
	29/12/16		Battn. in Front line Trenches.	
	30/12/16		2nd Lt. F.R. DIMOND reported for duty.	
	31/12/16		Battn. in Front Line Trenches. Authority given for Lieut. G.G. RYLANDS and 2nd Lieut. W.H. PIERCE to wear the badges of the rank of Captain, pending notification in the "London Gazette."	

Signed: L.H. Chapin
Major / Lt. Colonel
CO. 17th (SERVICE) BATT. THE LIVERPOOL REGT.

Stamp: 17TH (SERVICE) BATT. ORDERLY ROOM 3 JAN 1917 THE LIVERPOOL R

WAR DIARY
or
INTELLIGENCE SUMMARY
(Erase heading not required.)

Army Form C. 2118

Instructions regarding War Diaries and Intelligence Summaries are contained in F.S. Regs., Part II. and the Staff Manual respectively. Title Pages will be prepared in manuscript.

Place	Date	Hour	Summary of Events and Information	Remarks and references to Appendices
HUMBERCAMPS.	1/1/17	3 P.M.	Battalion relieved by 19th Battn. K.L.R. and moved into Billets in HUMBERCAMPS.	
- do -	2/1/17		REINFORCEMENT:- 9 Officers reported for duty.	
	3/1/17		Battalion in Reserve Billets. Spent day cleaning up. Battalion in Reserve Billets.	
	...	12. noon	Battalion paraded at very short notice, for Inspection by LORD DERBY, the Secretary of State for War, who complimented the Battalion on its turn-out at such very short notice, and after so trying a time in the Trenches.	
	4/1/17	2.45 P.M.	Battalion relieved 19th Battn. K.L.R. in "B.2" Subsector. Relief complete 3.45 P.M.	
	5/1/17		Battalion in Front Line Trenches.	
	6/1/17	12 noon	- do - Lt. Col. J.N. PECK returned from leave.	
	7/1/17	12 noon	Battalion relieved in "B.2" Subsector by 3/7th Bn. West Riding Regt., and marched to HUMBERCAMPS. Billeted in Camp "C".	
HUMBERCAMPS.	...	8 a.m.	Battn. marched from Huts Huts in HUMBERCAMPS to Huts in	
- do -	8/1/17	11.30 A.M.	HALLOY, arriving at 11.30 A.M.	
HALLOY.	...		Battn. in Camp "C". Spent day cleaning, refitting, bathing &c.	
- do -	9/1/17		- do -	
- do -	10/1/17		- do - Training, and Working Parties.	
- do -	11/1/17		- do - Training, and Working Parties.	
- do -	12/1/17		- do - Training :- Bayonet Fighting. Rifle Grenades. Bombers etc.	
- do -	13/1/17		- do - Training during the morning. Afternoon - Football. Reinforcement :- 2 Officers & 4 O.R. reported for duty.	

Army Form C. 2118

WAR DIARY
or
INTELLIGENCE SUMMARY

(Erase heading not required.)

Instructions regarding War Diaries and Intelligence Summaries are contained in F. S. Regs., Part II. and the Staff Manual respectively. Title Pages will be prepared in manuscript.

Place	Date	Hour	Summary of Events and Information	Remarks and references to Appendices
HALLOY	27/1/17	—	2 Companies engaged on Working Parties. Remainder of Battalion - Training - Physical Drill, Attack Practice &c.	
- do -	28/1/17	—	Battalion engaged on Working Parties - } Constructing new	
- do -	29/1/17	—	— do — } Railway Line.	
- do -	30/1/17	—	— do —	
- do -	31/1/17	—	2 Companies engaged on Working Parties. Remainder of Battalion - Attack Practice.	

J Welch
LIEUT. COLONEL
O.C. 17th (SERVICE) BATT. THE LIVERPOOL REGT

Vol 16

16.C.
4 sheets

CONFIDENTIAL.

War Diary.

of

17TH BATTALION KING'S LIVERPOOL REGIMENT.

FROM 1ST FEBRUARY 1917. TO 28TH FEBRUARY. 1917.

(VOLUME. 16.)

Army Form C. 2118

WAR DIARY
or
INTELLIGENCE SUMMARY
(Erase heading not required.)

Instructions regarding War Diaries and Intelligence Summaries are contained in F.S. Regs., Part II. and the Staff Manual respectively. Title Pages will be prepared in manuscript.

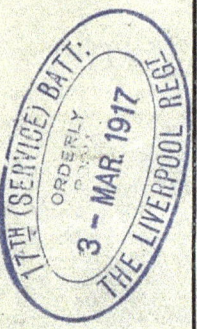

17TH (SERVICE) BATT:
ORDERLY ROOM
3 - MAR. 1917
THE LIVERPOOL REGT.

Place	Date	Hour	Summary of Events and Information	Remarks and references to Appendices
HALLOY	1/2/17		Battalion in Hutments. Engaged in Training & Working Parties.	
-do-	2/2/17		-do- -do-	
-do-	3/2/17		-do- -do-	
-do-	4/2/17		-do- -do-	
-do-	5/2/17	9.30am	Battn. marched from Hutments in HALLOY to SIMENCOURT.	
SIMENCOURT	-"-	3.45pm	Arrived in Billets.	
-do-	6/2/17	4.30pm	Battn. marched to ARRAS.	
ARRAS	-"-	7.30pm	Arrived in Billets.	
-do-	7/2/17		Battn. in Billets.	
-do-	8/2/17		-do- -do-	
-do-	9/2/17		-do- -do- Working Parties.	
-do-	10/2/17		-do- -do-	
-do-	11/2/17		-do- -do-	
-do-	12/2/17	9 am	Battn. commenced to move up to Front Line to relieve 19th Bn. K.L.R. in 'G' I. Right Subsection.	
-do-	-"-	12 noon	Relief complete. 1 OR. Wounded.	
-do-	13/2/17		Battn. in Front Line Trenches.	
-do-	14/2/17		-do- -do-	
-do-	15/2/17		-do- -do-	
-do-	16/2/17		-do- -do-	
-do-	17/2/17		-do- -do-	

WAR DIARY or INTELLIGENCE SUMMARY

Army Form C. 2118

(Erase heading not required.)

Place	Date	Hour	Summary of Events and Information	Remarks and references to Appendices
	19/2/17		Battn. in Front Line Trenches. Lt. Col. J.N. Peck proceeded on leave to U.K. Capt. C.E. Torrey assumed Temporary Command of Battalion. 2nd Lt. C.A. Peters returned for duty. CASUALTY: 1 O.R. wounded.	
	20/2/17		Battn. in Front Line Trenches.	
	21/2/17		-do-	
	22/2/17		-do-	
	23/2/17		-do-	
		9 PM	Small German Patrol was seen in our wire. Bombs were thrown & Lewis Gun opened fire, after which the patrol disappeared. One German however jumped into our Trench and was wounded in the shoulder, and man surrendered; he was escorted to Brigade Headquarters. Sentry fired at him & he surrendered, and after being dressed was escorted to the 102nd R.I.R. (Saxon). 23rd Reserve Division. The Prisoner belonged to the 102nd R.I.R. (Saxon). 23rd Reserve Division. Battn. in Front Line Trenches.	
	24/2/17	9.30 AM	A wounded German crawled into our Trenches. He had apparently been lying out all night in our wire. Prisoner was conveyed to Medical Aid Post to have wounds dressed, and proceeded	
		11.20 AM	Battn. was relieved by 2nd Bn. Bedfordshire Regt. and proceeded to Arras. Battn. in Billets. Engaged on Working Parties.	
ARRAS	25/2/17		-do- -do- -do-	
-do-	26/2/17		-do- -do- -do-	
-do-	27/2/17		-do- -do- -do-	
-do-	28/2/17		-do- -do- -do-	

J.M. Peck
COMDG 17/M (CERTIFIED BATT: THE LIVERPOOL REGT)

Vol 17.

17.C.
13 sheets

CONFIDENTIAL.

WAR DIARY

OF

17TH BATTALION. KING'S LIVERPOOL REGIMENT.

FROM 1st MARCH 1917. TO 31st MARCH 1917.

VOLUME 17.

FILE No. G. 12

Sub-Nos. 19,

SUBJECT. MINOR OPERATIONS.

Sub-head. Enemy Raid on

17th Bn King's Liverpool Regt.

8th March, 1917

Referred to.	Date.	Referred to.	Date.

WAR DIARY or INTELLIGENCE SUMMARY

Army Form C. 2118

(Erase heading not required.)

Instructions regarding War Diaries and Intelligence Summaries are contained in F.S. Regs., Part II. and the Staff Manual respectively. Title Pages will be prepared in manuscript.

Place	Date	Hour	Summary of Events and Information	Remarks and references to Appendices
ARRAS.	1/3/17		Battn. in Billets.	
	2/3/17	11.55AM	Lieut. A.V. COLLINS reported for duty. Battn. relieved 2nd B. Bedfordshire Regt. in "G.1. Rifle Subsector".	
	3/3/17		Battn. in Front Line Trenches.	
	4/3/17		-do- — 3 O.R. Wounded.	
	5/3/17		-do- — 1 O.R. Wounded.	
	6/3/17		-do- — 2 O.R. Reinforcement.	
	-"-		2 O.R. Killed in Action.	
	7/3/17		Battalion in Front Line Trenches.	
	8/3/17	4.15AM	-do- Enemy Raiding Party entered our Trenches, after a bombardment, and captured 4 men.	
	9/3/17		Battn. in Front Line Trenches.	
	10/3/17		-do-	
	11/3/17		-do-	
	12/3/17		-do-	
	13/3/17		-do-	
	-"-		2nd Lieut. Dy/F. BELLAMY transferred to Army Signal Service.	
	14/3/17		Battn. relieved by 19th K.L.R. in "G.1. Right Subsector".	
	-"-	2.30PM	Relief complete & moved into ARRAS.	

WAR DIARY or INTELLIGENCE SUMMARY

Army Form C. 2118

(Erase heading not required.)

Instructions regarding War Diaries and Intelligence Summaries are contained in F.S. Regs., Part II. and the Staff Manual respectively. Title Pages will be prepared in manuscript.

Place	Date	Hour	Summary of Events and Information	Remarks and references to Appendices
ARRAS	15/3/17		Battn. in Billets. Engaged on Working Parties.	
-do-	16/3/17		-do- -do-	
-do-	17/3/17		-do- -do-	
			Reinforcements 6 O.R.	
	18/3/17	2 P.M.	Battn. moved from ARRAS to RESERVE LINE, AGNY on account of German withdrawal	
	19/3/17		Battn. in RESERVE LINE. AGNY. Carrying Rations, etc to Front Line	
	20/3/17		-do- -do-	
	21/3/17		-do- -do-	
	22/3/17		-do- -do-	
AGNY.	23/3/17		Battn. moved from AGNY to BRETENCOURT + moved into old British Front Line.	
BRETENCOURT	24/3/17		Battn. marched from BRETENCOURT to BASSEUX.	
BASSEUX	25/3/17		Battn. march from BASSEUX to SAULTY.	
SAULTY.	26/3/17		Battn. in Billets. Course of Training at Divisional School.	
-do-	27/3/17			
	28/3/17			
	29/3/17			
	30/3/17			
	31/3/17			

A.H. Chadwick [?]
LIEUT. COLONEL
17th (SERVICE) BATT: THE LIVERPOOL REGT.

Third Army.

I forward herewith a report by the G.O.C. 30th Division on the small raid carried out by the enemy in M.14.c. in the early morning of the 8th instant.

I do not consider that any blame attaches to the officers on the spot. The possibility of a raid was foreseen, and adequate arrangements made to meet it.

The loss of the Lewis Gun must be ascribed to the rapidity of the enemy's movements and the failure of the two bombers, posted for the purpose, to warn the detachment.

9th March 1917.

Lieutenant-General,
Commanding VIIth Corps.

VIIth. Corps.

G.847.   8th. March, 1917.

I went down to the line this morning and personally investigated the case. I agree with the views expressed by Lieut. Col. H.S. Poyntz D.S.O., Commanding 89th. Infantry Brigade.

2/Lieut. Peters in my opinion did well.

HShea
Major General
30th. Division.   Commanding

89th Brigade No.B.156.

Head Quarters,
    30th Division.

Reference Raid made by the enemy into our trenches night of 7th/8th March 1917.

I forward herewith a report by Lieut Colonel Peck, Commanding 17th Battalion King's Liverpool Regt. into whose trenches the enemy entered.

On the afternoon of March 5th, the enemy heavily trench mortared our front line between Saps G.6 and G.9., blowing a gap of about 40 yards into our wire.

Suspecting this might lead to an enemy raid I immediately arranged with Lieut. Colonel Peck, that he should -

1. Wire up the Gap as soon as possible.

2. Vacate the front line at this point except for a double Sentry to watch the gap in the wire. If the enemy were observed coming across, they were to open fire and fire a Very light, and retire to LITTLE GEM STREET. This they did with the exception of the Very Light, for some reason the pistol would not work.

3. Place Lewis Guns on the flanks of the Gap with a strong Block of Bombers in the main trench to cover the gunners. Unfortunately I did not state the number and only two bombers were put to protect the right gun. If the enemy were in too great numbers these guns and bombers were to withdraw up GEORGE STREET and LITTLE GEM STREET.

4. Immediately the enemy put up a barrage the Lewis Guns were to bring a Cross Fire on to the neutral ground in front of the gap and also the gun in the Support Line as on sketch.

5. Place bombing blocks in GEORGE STREET and GEM STREET in case enemy tried to get into the Support line.

6. Organize the Support Platoon so as to be ready for immediate counter-attack.

On examination of the ground to-day, I found that the enemy had not entered by the gap which had been nearly all rewired, but they cut the wire halfway down Sap G.6.a. on the East side and got into the sap, working down the Sap into the front line trench and up towards GEORGE STREET. They had marked this gap for returning, by hanging bomb bags on the wire with safety pins.

I am inclined to think that the two bombers who were posted in the front trench east of GEORGE STREET to protect the Lewis Gunners, must have lain in the bottom of the trench during the barrage and could not have looked over the top, or down the main trench to see what was happening. Had they done so they could have warned the Lewis Gunners and covered their withdrawal up GEORGE ST.

H. S. Poyntz
    Lieut. Colonel.
Commanding 89th Infantry Brigade.

8/3/1917.

REPORT ON GERMAN RAID.

8th March 1917.

Head Quarters,

    89th Infantry Brigade.

    I regret to report that a GERMAN party entered my trenches this morning.

    At 4.5 a.m. the sentries in G.6a saw a GERMAN patrol about 6 strong on the left of the sap. They fired and attempted to fire a Very Light which failed. In accordance with orders they retired via LITTLE GEM STREET to the SUPPORT LINE on the way seeing another GERMAN party about the same strength to the right of Sap G.6a. They warned the garrison of LITTLE GEM STREET and went round to GEORGE STREET. At 4.5 a.m. the GERMANS opened a barrage on the FRONT and SUPPORT LINE, but mostly on the SUPPORT LINE (probably SHORTS only on the FRONT LINE). Immediately the barrage opened the line stood-to. Apparently the raiding party worked very quickly to the right capturing the two sentries of the bombing post 4 bays to the left of GEORGE STREET and the two sentries and LEWIS GUN one bay to the left of GEORGE STREET. Then they retired straight to their own line, again under fire on their way back. Apparently some of the enemy were hit as a GERMAN rifle and bags of bombs were picked up in the wire left of G.6a. A Very Light pistol and bomb bags can be seen lying outside. A GERMAN jumping the trench at GEORGE STREET was also wounded but got away. The GERMAN barrage consisted of Medium Trench Mortars and 77 mm. and was not very heavy. It included the RESERVE LINE. I rang up C.149 when it started and asked for retaliation in case it might mean anything. The sentries captured had just gone on post at 4 a.m. when all was reported quiet.

    2nd Lieut. PETERS arrived at the head of GEORGE STREET within 5 minutes of the barrage opening. The Germans had then retired. They were not in the line more than five minutes.

    This part of the line was held as per attached sketch.

(Signed.)   J. N. PECK.

Lieut. Colonel.
17th Bn. Kings Liverpool Regiment.

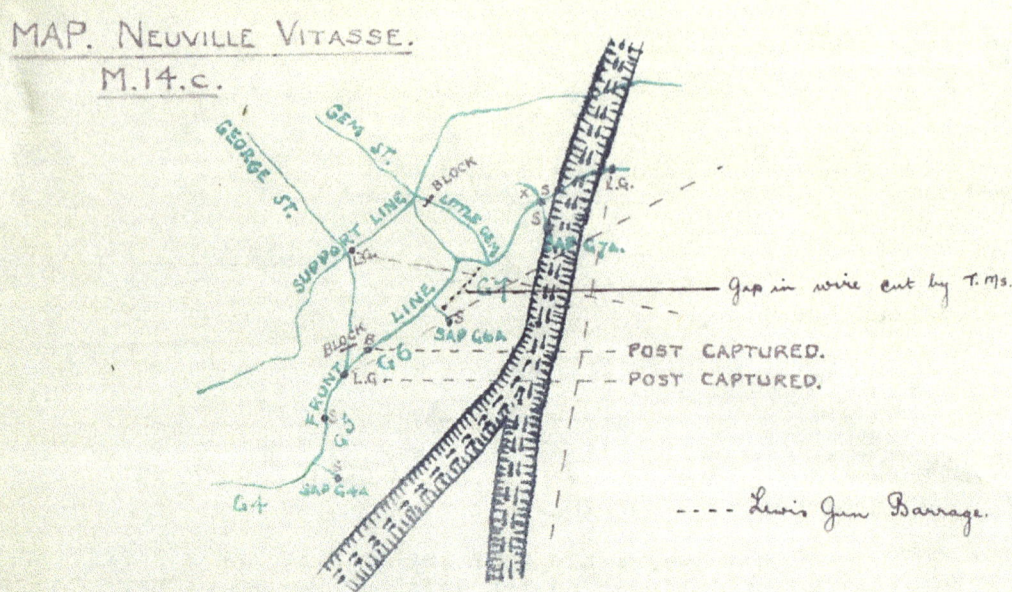

Section of Line G.1. Right Subsector, shewing posts.

Lewis Gun Posts marked   "L.G."

Bombing Posts. marked.   "B".

Sentry Posts marked   "S".

Russian Sap   "X".

****

Blocks at top of GEORGE STREET and near Support Line in LITTLE GEM STREET.

GEM STREET blocked up by T.Ms.

From G.7a. to GEORGE STREET trench had been cleared owing to damage to trench and wire by hostile T.Ms. on 5th instant and in contemplation of a Raid by the enemy.

8/3/1917.

"C" Form (Original).
MESSAGES AND SIGNALS.

Army Form C. 2123.

Prefix	Code	Words 57	Received From	Sent, or sent out At ... m.	Office Stamp
Charges to collect			By	To ... By	
Service Instructions.	Priority				

Handed in at **6co.** Office **9.35** m. Received **9.42** m.

TO Third Army.

Sender's Number	Day of Month	In reply to Number	AAA
G.620	Eighth		

30 Div report AAA Enemy opened barrage 4.10 am on front line GEM to GATE STREET AAA 4 men of Lewis Gun Team 17 Liverpool posted 4 AM and heard firing during barrage AAA. Visited by an officer during barrage at 4.15 am and found missing with gun.

FROM PLACE & TIME 7 Corps. 9.30 am.

GA5K

Vol 18

18.C
6 sheets

CONFIDENTIAL.

WAR DIARY.

of

17TH BATTALION. KING'S LIVERPOOL REGIMENT.

FROM 1ST APRIL 1917. TO 30TH APRIL 1917.

VOLUME No. 18

WAR DIARY or INTELLIGENCE SUMMARY

Army Form C. 2118

(Erase heading not required.)

Instructions regarding War Diaries and Intelligence Summaries are contained in F.S. Regs., Part II. and the Staff Manual respectively. Title Pages will be prepared in manuscript.

Place	Date	Hour	Summary of Events and Information	Remarks and references to Appendices
SAULTY	1/4/17	9.00 a.m.	The half battalion at the Divisional School marched to rejoin the other half at BAVINCOURT.	
BAVINCOURT	2/4/17	11.00 a.m.	Bn. practised mopping up.	
	3/4/17	4.45 p.m.	Bn. marched to BLAIRVILLE QUARRY (3 coys) & FICHEUX (1 coy) and came into reserve to 90th Bde.	
BLAIRVILLE & FICHEUX	4/4/17 5 6 7		Bn. in reserve to 90th Bde. One coy in strong points east of ARRAS–ALBERT railway north of BOISLEUX-AU-MONT. Remainder of Bn. working parties and mopping up practices.	
— do —	8/4/17	7.0 p.m.	Bn. marched to take up assembly positions for attack. Disposition:– Bn. Headquarters and A & C coys in Bois nunnun in sunken road running N. from BOISLEUX-AU-MONT. B & D coys dug in west of BOIRY COPSE (W of HENIN) Mopping up HINDENBURG LINE and HENINEL for Armentines Bns. 19th K.L.R. (right) 20th K.L.R. (left). Bn. assembling east of Bois in trenches behind HENIN. All in position by 12 mn.	
Sunken road N of BOISLEUX	9/4/17	5.30 a.m.	Zero for whole attack.	
		3.6 p.m.	Armentines nunnun & moppers advanced to attack. Whole Bde. were never advancing. Attack held up by machine gun situation extreme.	
		6.20 p.m.	Ordered to nun one company to trenches vacated by 1st nunn W of HENIN.	
		6.35 p.m.	A coy moved up.	
		9.50 p.m.	B & D coys ordered to reform on original positions behind BOIRY COPSE.	

Army Form C. 2118

WAR DIARY
or
INTELLIGENCE SUMMARY
(Erase heading not required.)

Instructions regarding War Diaries and Intelligence Summaries are contained in F.S. Regs., Part II. and the Staff Manual respectively. Title Pages will be prepared in manuscript.

Place	Date	Hour	Summary of Events and Information	Remarks and references to Appendices
Sunken Road N/E BOISLEUX	9.4.17	10.0 p.m	Bn H.Q. & C Coy mard forward H.Q to NAGPUR TRENCH. C Coy to Sunken road N of BOIRY BECQUERELLE.	
NAGPUR TRENCH	10.4.17	12.0 m.n.	Situation :- H.Q in NAGPUR TRENCH. B.C. & D Coys in BOIRY BECQUERELLE. A Coy Trenches W of HENIN. Casualties 2nd Lt. B.S. DAVIS comdg B Coy Killed. - A.R. CARR killed. Wounded 2nd Lt. E.H. BENNETT, 2nd Lt. MAHON 2nd Lt. G.L. KEY. 16 O.R. Killed 48 O.R. wounded. The 1st Bn. O/ficers were all the O/ficers in action with B. Coy.	
— do —	10.4.17		Remained in Sunken Road.	
— do —	11.4.17	4.0 a.m	Mard A Coy to Sunken road running N from ST MARTIN	
		6.0 a.m	2nd Bn. Bedfordshire Reg.t & 20th Bn Kings L. Reg.t attack endeavoured to unite HINDENBURG LINE Through gaps in wire. Attack failed.	
— do — N. of HENIN	11.4.17	10.30 a.m	Remainder of Bn mard up to Sunken road N from ST MARTIN and NAGPUR TRENCH S.W. of Thin. Bn H.Q. in NAGPUR TRENCH N.W. of HENIN.	
	11.4.17	2.0 p.m	Patrol sent forward into Hindenburg line made connection with 17th M.C. who had occupied line after 5.5 Div. from left hand trench	

2nd Lt. H.L. GARDNER wounded

Army Form C. 2118

WAR DIARY
or
INTELLIGENCE SUMMARY
(Erase heading not required.)

Instructions regarding War Diaries and Intelligence Summaries are contained in F.S. Regs., Part II. and the Staff Manual respectively. Title Pages will be prepared in manuscript.

Place	Date	Hour	Summary of Events and Information	Remarks and references to Appendices
BLAIRVILLE	12.4.17	4.0 p.m.	Relieved by 2nd Bn. Royal Welsh Fusiliers & marched to our Billets near BLAIRVILLE arriving about 8.0 p.m.	
BAILLEULVAL	13.4.17	9.0 a.m.	Bn. marched to BAILLEULVAL	
"	13.4.17	11.30 a.m.	In Billets	
"	14.4.17	4.0 p.m.	Bn. marched to COUIN	
COUIN	14.4.17	8.15 p.m.	Bn. in Billets	
"	15.4.17		" " refitting. Rein. joining to 34 O.R.	
"	16.4.17		Bn. in Billets training	
			Lieut. A. CHAVASSE reported from 11th Bn. R.L.R. reported for duty 22nd Lt W.E. HEATH on appointment reported for duty.	
"	17.4.17 18.4.17 19.4.17		Bn. in Billets training	
"	20.4.17	8.00 a.m.	Bn. entrained to go to BEAURAINS. Detrained at DAINVILLE	
BEAURAINS	20.4.17	6.0 p.m.	Bn. in old German lines (X works) at BEAURAINS.	
"	21.4.17 22.4.17		" "	
"	23.4.17	3.30 p.m.	Brigade in reserve. O returned to man in mainly to NEUVILLE VITASSE	
NEUVILLE VITASSE		5.15 p.m.	arrived in to HINDENBURG system	

Army Form C. 2118

WAR DIARY
or
INTELLIGENCE SUMMARY
(Erase heading not required.)

Instructions regarding War Diaries and Intelligence Summaries are contained in F.S. Regs., Part II. and the Staff Manual respectively. Title Pages will be prepared in manuscript.

Place	Date	Hour	Summary of Events and Information	Remarks and references to Appendices
E of HENINEL	23.4.17	8.50 p.m	Bn. moved to position E of HENINEL to support 2/21st Inf. Bde.	
	24.4.17	2.00 a.m	arrived in position. HQ N 29 c 6/3	
		3.20 a.m	2/1st Bde. having moved forward Bn occupied their assigned line.	
N 29 a 1/3		1.20 p.m	Ordered to support 2/21st Bde.	
		3.20 p.m	In position. Moved through considerable M.G. and canister Casualties 1 O.R. Killed 8 O.R. wounded	
	25.4.17	10.0 p.m	Moved A & C Coys to relieve two Coys of 2nd YORK'S in front line of pt. of CHERISY. HQ moved to quarry in N 30 b.	
N 30 b.	25.4.17	11.30 p.m	Reliefs complete. Bn relief in anticipation of making an attack on CHERISY. Casualties 5 O.R. wounded	
	26.4.17 27.4.17		Consolidation. attack cancelled & Bn am to be relieved. 2 O.R. Killed 4. O.R. wounded 10 O.R. wounded.	
	28.4.17	3.00 a.m	Attack by troops on our flanks. Barrage on our lines 10 O.R. wounded	
		10.15 p.m	Reliefs of A B C by 7th Bn East Yorkshire Regt — & B & D by 12th Bn Middlesex commenced	
		11.50 p.m	Reliefs complete. Bn moved to HINDENBURG system W of WANCOURT LINE	
HINDENBURG SYSTEM	29th	7.00 a.m	Arrived 3.0 a.m. Casualties 2 Lt L. BAND & 11 O.R. killed 11 O.R. wounded. Bn moved to BEAVRAINS Then To ARRAS and entrained at 2.0 p.m	
			To P.C. HOUVAIN	
HAUTE-COTE	29th	8.45 p.m	arrived in billets at HAUTE-COTE	
—"—	30th		In billets. Refitting.	

J.W. Peck

LIEUT. COLONEL
COMD'G. 17TH (SERVICE) BATT. THE LIVERPOOL REGT

SECRET   COPY NO 5

OPERATION ORDER NO. 56 BY LIEUT.COL.J.N.PECK.M.C.
COMMANDING 17TH BATTN. KING'S LIVERPOOL REGT.

                                                    Headquarters,
                                                    7th April 1917.

Reference Map:-   51b. S.W. (1/20,000).

1.   The Third Army will attack on April 9th 1917.

2. OBJECTIVES. The 89th Infantry Brigade will attack:-
   (a).   The German System of trenches known as the COJEUL SWITCH from
          the junction of NATAL TRENCH with the German Front Line (N.27.9/5)
          to the junction of the German front line with the HENIN - HENINEL
          road (exclusive) at N.34.a.75/70.
   (b).   The village of HENINEL.
   (c).   The high ground in N.30.a. & b., and N.24.d.

3. TROOPS ON FLANK. The 21st Division will be on the right of the
   Brigade. The Battalion on our immediate right being 9th Battalion
   K.O.Y.L.I. (IRON), 64th Infantry Brigade (BITS).
                The 21st Infantry Brigade will be on the left. The
   right Battalion of that Brigade will be the 2nd Battalion Wiltshire
   Regt.

4. BOUNDARIES. The boundaries of the Brigade are as shewn on the
   attached map "A".

5. DISPOSITION. The attack will be carried out by 19th Battalion
   K.L.R. (on the right) and the 20th Battalion K.L.R. (on the left).
                The dividing line will be as shewn on the attached
   map "A".
                The 2nd.Bn.Bedfordshire Regt. will be in Support.
                The 17th Battalion K.L.R. will be in Reserve, and
   will provide mopping up and carrying parties as detailed in paras.
   7 and 16.
                The 19th and 20th Battalions K.L.R. will each have
   2 Companies in front, and 2 Companies in Support. The 2 leading
   Companies of each Battalion will each have 2 Platoons in the first
   wave, and 2 Platoons in the second wave.
                The 19th Battalion K.L.R. will have 3 Companies on
   the right (South) bank of the River COJEUL, and 1 Companies on the
   left (North) bank.
                The O.C., 2nd Bn. Bedfordshire Regt. will detail 2
   Companies for the support of the 19th Battalion K.L.R.
                These Companies will cross the river at HENIN and
   will closely support the Company of 19th Battalion K.L.R. ~~North
   of the River COJEUL~~ on the South Bank of the River COJEUL.
                He will also detail 1 Company for the support of the
   20th Battalion K.L.R. and the Company of 19th Battalion K.L.R.
   North of the River COJEUL.
                The fourth Company will remain in the hands of the
   O.C., 2nd Bn.Bedfordshire Regt.

6. ASSEMBLY.   The Brigade will assemble as follows:-

   19th Battalion K.L.R.

        Battalion H.Q.   T.1.a.10/15.
        4 Platoons (first wave) in trenches from about T.2.a.7/3 to
                about T.2.b.1/2.
        8 Platoons (second wave of leading Companies and first wave
                of Supporting Companies) in sunken roads from T.1.c.6/6
                Southwards.
                (To dig in on each side of road).
        4 Platoons (second wave of Support Companies) to dig in in the
                ploughed field from S.11.b.9/9 Southwards.

   20th Battalion K.L.R.

6. **ASSEMBLY** (cont.)

   20th Battalion K.L.R.

   Battalion H.Q.　　　　S.6.b.9/1.
   4 Platoons (first wave) in trench from about T.2.a.5/4
       to about T.2.a.2/7.
   8 Platoons (second wave of leading Companies and first
       wave of supporting Companies) in sunken road
       from T.1.c.6/6 Northwards.
       (To dig in on each side of the road).
   4 Platoons (second wave of Support Companies) in SWITCH
       LANE from S.11.b.25/95 Southwards.

   2nd. Bn. Bedfordshire Regt.

   Battalion H.Q.　　　　S.11.b.4/7.
   Whole battalion in SWITCH LANE from M.35.c.3/0 Southwards
       to S.11.b.25/95.

   17th Battalion K.L.R.

   Battalion H.Q.　　　　S.4.c.8/1.
   7 Platoons in sunken road from that point Northwards
       (5 Platoons "C" Coy. on Left. - "A" Coy. on Right).
   6 Platoons in NAGPUR TRENCH from T.1.a.3/3 Eastwards.

   89th Machine Gun Company.

   H.Q. and ½ section in sunken road from S.R.c.5/1 to
       point where road cuts railway at S.10.a.6/6.
   1 Section in trench on road M.35.c.2/7.
   ¼ Section with 19th Battalion K.L.R.
   ¼ Section with 20th Battalion K.L.R.
   ¼ Section with 2nd Bn.Bedfordshire Regt.
   1 Section holding present line.

   89th Trench Mortar Battery.

   Sunken Road from S.11.a.45/80 Southwards.

   89th Brigade Pioneer Company.

   Railway cutting from S.10.a.6/6 to the South East.

   All troops will be in position by midnight April 8th/9th 1917.

7. **MOPPERS UP.**　　The 17th Battalion K.L.R. will furnish the
following mopping up parties:-
   (a). "B" Company to deal with the front and support lines of the
       COJEUL SWITCH and the sunken road running between them, from the
       left boundary of the Brigade to the River COJEUL.
   (b). 2 Platoons of "D" Company to deal with the front and support
       lines of the COJEUL SWITCH from the River COJEUL to the right
       boundary of the Brigade.
   (c). 2 Platoons of "D" Company to deal with the village of HENINEL.
       This party will follow the fourth wave of the attack North of
       the River COJEUL, and will deal with that portion of HENINEL
       North West of the River.

   The 2 Platoons detailed under (b) will deal with that portion
   of HENINEL South East of the River.
   On completion of their task, all mopping parties will withdraw to
   NAGPUR TRENCH (N.32.b). and report arrival to Battn.H.Q.

AMENDMENT TO OPERATION ORDER NO. 56.

Headquarters,
7th April 1917.

Reference Map :- 51b. S.W. (1/20,000).

1. Operation Order No. 56, para. 6, ASSEMBLY, as relating to 17th K.L.R. is cancelled and the following substituted :-

    17th Battn. K.L.R.

    Battn. H.Q.   S. 4.c.8/1.
    7 Platoons in sunken road, from Battn. H.Q. Northwards (3 Platoons of "C" Coy. on Left, - "A" Coy. on Right).
    "B" Coy. & 2 Platoons "D" Coy. will dig in about the line, T.1.a.5/3 to T.1.d.0/3.
    2 Platoons of "D" Coy. will dig in about the line T.1.d.0/3 to T.1.d.2/0.
    Sections will dig in together, and dig narrow trenches, all the earth to be well scattered and levelled down.
    No movement or digging to take place between daybreak and the advance.

2. **POWER BUZZER.** L/Corpl G.W. JONES and 3 Signallers will report at Battn. H.Q. at 6.30 p.m. and then proceed to take over Power Buzzer Set at T.1.a.1/2.
    Taking over to be complete by 8 p.m.

3. **STRAGGLERS POST.** O.C. H.Q. Company will detail 3 of the Police, (N.C.O. in charge), for duty at Stragglers Post at S.11.c.6/9. They will proceed to take over immediately after dinners. Blankets will be taken.

4. **MOPPERS UP.** 2 Candles and 1 Box of Matches will be carried by each man.

[signature]

Lieut. & Adjutant.
17th Battn. K.L.R.

SUPPLEMENT TO OPERATION ORDER No. 56. - 17th K.L.R.

ACTION OF MACHINE GUNS.

1. There will be no machine gun covering fire.

2. One Section of the 89th Machine Gun Coy. will advance on the right flank of the 21st Infantry Brigade, and immediately after their leading waves, and will establish themselves on the Southern slope of the spur running through N.26.c. central, and N.26.b.5/0, from which positions they will be able to bring fire on the Southern portion of the HINDENBURG LINE to be attacked by the Brigade, during its advance.

   Half a Section will also be attached to the Left Battalion to form part of a garrison of strong points in or about the HINDENBURG Line.

   Half a Section will be attached to the Right Battalion.
   Half a Section will be attached to the Support Battalion.

3. During the advance to the "Green line", the section of Machine Guns mentioned in 2. para. 1. will move forward to a point, roughly about N.22.d.4/0, in order that they may bring fire to bear up the valley of the River COJEUL towards WANCOURT, and up the slopes towards the "Green line".

   The half section attached to the right battalion will move to a point near the cross roads in N.29.a. for the purpose of shooting up the valley towards GUEMAPPE.

   The half-section attached to the Support Battalion will move to a position about N.29.c.0/4 in order to safe-guard the right flank of the Brigade, against counter-attack in the case of the Division on the right not having progressed.

Issued to Runner at 11.30. p.m., 7.4.1917.

Copy No. 1. Retained.
2. H.Q. 89th Infantry Brigade.
3. O.C., 19th Battn. K.L.R.
4. O.C., 20th Battn. K.L.R.
5. O.C., 2nd Bn. Bedfordshire Regt.
6. O.C., "A" Company.
7. O.C., "B" Company.
8. O.C., "C" Company.
9. O.C., "D" Company.
10. O.C., H.Q.Company.
11. Medical Officer.
12. Quartermaster.
13. Transport Officer.
14. Regl. Sergt. Major.
15. War Diary.

4.

9. **INFANTRY ADVANCES (cont.)**

(e). The Royal Engineers will construct strong points at N.36.b.4/6, N.34.c.5/3, N.34.b.2/1, N.18.d.4/1, the two former of which are in the 89th Brigade area and will be manned.
The R.E. will also prepare HENINEL for defence.

(f). The 21st Division will advance simultaneously with the 89th Infantry Brigade.

(g). Previous to this operation ST. MARTIN-SUR-COJEUL will have been captured.

10. **HOURS OF ADVANCE.** The following table gives the times at which troops should leave their Assembly Positions, calculated so as to give the correct distances between waves, and to bring the leading wave within 2 minutes of the barrage :-

19th Battalion K.L.R.

1st Wave	leaves its position at	ZERO plus 8 hours 36 minutes.
2nd Wave	: : :	ZERO plus 8 hours 6 minutes.
3rd Wave	: : :	ZERO plus 9 hours 7 minutes.
4th Wave	: : :	ZERO plus 8 hours 22 minutes.

20th Battalion K.L.R.

1st Wave	leaves its position at	ZERO plus 9 hours 37 minutes.
2nd Wave	: : :	ZERO plus 8 hours 10 minutes.
3rd Wave	: : :	ZERO plus 9 hours 11 minutes.
4th Wave	: : :	ZERO plus 8 hours 25 minutes.

17th Battalion K.L.R. (moppers up) will fit in , in front of the Waves they should precede, i.e.,
2 plats."B" Coy. & 1 plat."D" Co. Moppers for front line & C.Ts.
behind 1st Wave.
2 plats."B" Coy. & 1 plat."D" Co. Moppers for Support Line
behind 2nd Wave.
2 plats."D" Coy. Moppers for HENINEL behind 4th Wave.
Movement by sections in file as long as possible.

11. **89th MACHINE GUN COY.** The 89th Machine Gun Coy. will act according to B. 299 of March 31st which has been issued to all concerned.
The section of guns now in the line will remain in their positions after the troops have passed through.

12. **89th TRENCH MORTAR BATTERY.** The 89th Trench Mortar Battery will place two guns at the disposal of the O.C. 19th Battalion K.L.R. and 2 guns at the disposal of the O.C., 20th Battalion K.L.R.
These guns will be moved forward under the orders of Os.C. above Battalions.
The teams of the remaining four guns will provide the necessary carrying parties.

13. **FLANK PARTIES.** The O.C.,,20th Battalion K.L.R. will detail a Bombing Party to work up NAGPUR TRENCH and NATAL TRENCH in conjunction with the advance of the 21st Infantry Brigade in order to protect its flank.
Similarly, other bombing parties will work up the sunken Road from N.33.c.9/6 to N.26.c.0/7, and along the ST. MARTIN - NEUVILLE VITASSE road, through N.35.d. up to N.36. central.
On the advance of the 89th Infantry Brigade these parties will rejoin their Battalion.

14. **CAVALRY.** After the capture of HENINEL and WANCOURT it is probable that Cavalry will pass through our lines and form a screen about the "Green line" on the crest of the hill.

15. **CARRYING PARTIES:** 1 Platoon of "C" Company, 17th Battalion K.L.R., under an Officer, will report to 89th Machine-Gun Coy. Headquarters

19. **INTELLIGENCE (Cont.).**

desirable.
  (c). Officers and men will be separated at once on capture.
  Officers and N.C.Os. will be searched for documents at once; men will **NOT** be searched till they reach the Corps Cage.
  All documents will be sent <u>with</u> the prisoners to the Joint Divisional Cage.

  (d). Two special Intelligence men each will be detailed by O.C. "D" & O.C. "B" Coys. and will accompany Os.C. these Coys. They will wear a black armband marked "I" and withdraw carry sacks to contain letters, documents, and maps. These sacks will be labelled with a black band or patch.
  Their duty is to collect documents out of dugouts, off dead officers, etc., and send them back with prisoners' escorts to Battn. H.Q.
  If an Intelligence man, or any man, carrying one of these sacks becomes a casualty, it is the duty of any Officer to order another man to take the sack.

  (e). All reports of prisoners captured will state the numeral on their shoulder straps.   Distinction must be made between I.R. and R.I.R.
  If prisoners are required for Stretcher parties, etc., at least two of each new unit should be sent to the Cage.
  Prisoners will be taken to the Advanced Collecting Station at S.3.5.3/5.

20. **DUMPS.**   The Brigade Dump will be at S.11.b.65/90.
  Small Advance Dump at S.6.E.5/0 under 2nd Lt. W.B. HOLME.
  Advance Dump - 200th Field Coy. R.E. at S.11.b.8/6.
  Water Dump - Battalion H.Q.

21. **MEDICAL ARRANGEMENTS.**   Advanced Dressing Station at S.5.a.0/5.
  Collecting Stations at S.5.d.8/1 and N.35.a.4/9.
  Regimental Aid Posts near to Battalion Headquarters.

22. **S.O.S.**   The S.O.S. signal will be a succession of Green Lights.

23. **SITUATION REPORTS.**   Situation reports will be rendered by Companies at 5 a.m., 8 a.m., etc., until ZERO plus 6 hours. After that they will be rendered at ZERO plus 7 hours, ZERO plus 8 hours, etc.

24. **ZERO.**   The hour of ZERO will be communicated at a later date.

25. **BRIGADE H.Q.**   Brigade Headquarters will be in the Railway Cutting N.3.a.7/7.

26. **PLEASE ACKNOWLEDGE.**

  [signature]

  Lieut. & Adjutant.
  17th Battn. A.I.F.

This copy of Operation Order must be handed in to H.Q. before moving up to final Assembly positions.

5.

15. CARRYING PARTIES (cont.).

by 8 p.m. April 8th 1917 to act as a Carrying party.

At ZERO plus 9 hours, the remainder of 17th Battalion K.L.R. will move to SWITCH LANE from the River COJEUL Northwards, and will hold themselves in readiness to provide large Carrying Parties.

Move by Sections in Artillery formation. Route to be reconnoitred after arrival in Assembly Position.

16. TANKS. It is probable that two Tanks will work down the COJEUL SWITCH from the left, and assist in the clearing up of the German system of trenches after their capture.

They will also probably co-operate in the capture of HENINEL.

One Section of "A" Coy., 17th Battn. K.L.R. will report at 3 p.m. Z - 1 day (April 8th), at road junction of M.29.c.1/5 (MERCATEL), and accompany them throughout the operations for the purpose of clearing wounded from their path, etc.

There are NO signals between Tanks and Infantry.

17. DISTINGUISHING FLAGS & DISCS. For purpose of co-operation with Artillery every Company and Platoon will carry a red & yellow diagonal flag. These flags are NOT to be stuck in the ground and will only mean anything when waved.

These flags will, except in emergency, only be shown by order of a Platoon Commander at special times and places.

Their capture by the enemy might cause serious trouble, and it is a matter of honour for a Platoon not to lose its flag.

Flags will not be carried by the 17th Battn. K.L.R.

Bombing parties will carry a small edition of the same flag.

The following signals will be used by the other Divisions of the VII Corps to mark the advance of leading Infantry :-

Right flank. (21st Divn.).	NIL.
Left flank (56th Divn.).	Yellow flag with black St. George's cross.
Left flank of 50 Divn. (14th Division).	Artillery boards top half red, lower half yellow. Also white boards with black diagonal cross at cross roads, etc., as reference points for Artillery.
The Cavalry Corps.	Will use small Red & White flags to denote positions of advanced detachments.

18. ARTILLERY. The Brigade will be covered by the Right Group, 30th Divisional Artillery, Commanded by Lieut.Col. LIVINGSTONE-LEARMONTH, 149th Brigade R.F.A.; H.Q. with 89th Brigade H.Q.

19. INTELLIGENCE. (a). Companies will take steps to obtain and will pass on to Battalion H.Q., the earliest possible information as to Units (Regiment, Battalion, and Company) to which enemy dead and prisoners belong.

This information is NOT to be delayed pending search for further details.

(b). It is the special task of all Intelligence Officers to obtain information as regards the enemy and to pass it on.

Battalion and Battery H.Q. should be located and searched at once. A Battalion and Company H.Q. are in dugouts in the second line of COJEUL SWITCH, just South of River COJEUL.

Information and documents it is particularly desired to obtain :-

   (i). Position of hostile batteries.
  (ii). Telephone message book.
 (iii). Ammunition states.
  (iv). Maps and sketches.

Prisoners from Pioneers and Gunners are especi...

Vol 19 ⁽³⁾

19.C
5 sheets

CONFIDENTIAL.

WAR DIARY.

OF

17th BN. "THE KINGS" (LIVERPOOL REGIMENT).

FROM: 1st MAY 1917.   TO: 31st MAY 1917.

(VOLUME 19).

Army Form C. 2118

WAR DIARY
or
INTELLIGENCE SUMMARY
(Erase heading not required.)

Instructions regarding War Diaries and Intelligence Summaries are contained in F.S. Regs., Part II. and the Staff Manual respectively. Title Pages will be prepared in manuscript.

Place	Date	Hour	Summary of Events and Information	Remarks and references to Appendices
HAUTE-COTE.	1.5.17		Battalion in Billets at HAUTE-COTE. Work:- Sectional Instruction and Arm Drill.	
" "	2.5.17	2.0 PM	Capt. W.H. PIERCE returned from Hospital & assumed command of "B" Coy. Battalion engaged in Drilling and Sectional Instruction.	
" "	3.5.17		Battalion marched to FORTEL.	
FORTEL	" "	3.50 PM	Battn. arrived in Billets.	
" "	4.5.17	10 AM	Battalion paraded for Route March. Classes for Instruction in Lewis Gun, Bombing, Rifle Grenades, Bayonet Fighting and Signalling commenced.	
" "	5.5.17	7.30 AM	Battalion marched to Brigade Training area. Companies engaged in Attack Practice, Arm Drill & Bayonet Fighting, during the day.	
" "	6.5.17	9 AM	"A" & "B" Companies marched off for practice on Rifle Range. Remainder of Battn. - Church Parades.	
" "	" "	1 PM	"A", "B", "C" & "A" Companies marched to Brigade Sports at BUIRE-AU-BOIS.	
" "	7.5.17	7.30 AM	Battalion marched to Brigade Training area for Company Attack Practice. Instructional Classes held as usual on Battn. Training Ground.	
" "	8.5.17	9 AM	"C" & "D" Companies marched off for Practice on Rifle Range. Remainder of Battn. - Squad, Arm + Gas Drill on Battn. Training Ground. Instructional Classes held as usual.	
" "	9.6.17	7.30 AM	Battalion marched to Brigade Training Area for Battn. Drill and Attack Practice.	
" "	10.5.17	9 AM	"A" & "B" Coys marched off for Practice on Rifle Range. "C" & "A" Coys - Mining Practice, Arm + Squad Drill on Battn. Training Ground. Instructional Classes on Battn. Training Ground.	
" "	11.5.17	7 AM	Battalion marched to VAULX for Brigade Training Operations.	
" "	12.5.17	7 AM	Battalion marched to area between BUIRE-AU-BOIS and VAULX. Paraded for Inspection by Lieut. Gen. H.E. WATTS, C.B. C.M.G. Comdg. XIX Corps.	

Army Form C. 2118

WAR DIARY
or
INTELLIGENCE SUMMARY
(Erase heading not required.)

Instructions regarding War Diaries and Intelligence Summaries are contained in F.S. Regs., Part II. and the Staff Manual respectively. Title Pages will be prepared in manuscript.

Place	Date	Hour	Summary of Events and Information	Remarks and references to Appendices
FORT EL.	13.5.17	—	Church Parade.	
—"—	14.5.17	3 P.M.	Battalion Sports held in field outside of Village.	
—"—	—"—	—	Battalion marched (by Companies) to Baths at FROHEN-LE-GRAND.	
—"—	—"—	2 P.M.	Battn marched to Bivouacs near BACHIMONT.	
BACHIMONT.	15.5.17	7.30 A.M.	Move completed — all Companies having arrived in camp.	
—"—	—"—	9.30 A.M.	Battalion proceeded to Brigade Training area for Advance Guard and Open Fighting Practice.	
—"—	16.5.17	—	"C" + "A" - practised on Rifle Range from 8 A.M. to 12 noon.	
—"—	—"—	—	"B" + "D" -do-	
—"—	—"—	—	"A" - Arm Drill + Sectional Instruction.	
—"—	—"—	3 P.M.	Brigade Sports held near BUIRE-AU-BOIS.	
BACHIMONT.	17.5.17	11 A.M.	Battalion marched to LE PONCHEL - VAULX area to seen new Billets.	
LE PONCHEL. VAULX	—"—	1 P.M.	"A" Company - in VAULX. and remainder of Battn. in LE PONCHEL. Move completed.	
—"—	18.6.17	9 A.M.	Battalion marched by Companies to Baths at WILLENCOURT.	
—"—	—"—	2.30 P.M.	"B" "C" + "D" Companies - Attack Practice on Battn. Training Ground.	
—"—	—"—	—	"A" Company - Sectional Instruction.	
—"—	19.5.17	8.30 A.M.	Battalion marched to Brigade Training Ground for Attack and Field Firing Practice with live ammunition. Stokes Guns co-operated in the operations.	
—"—	20.5.17	9 A.M.	Battalion marched to Billets at HAUTE-COTE.	
HAUTE-COTE.	—"—	1.40 P.M.	Arrived in Billets.	
—"—	21.5.17	8.15 A.M.	Battalion marched to Billets at VALHOUN.	
VALHOUN.	—"—	2 P.M.	Battalion arrived in Billets.	

Army Form C. 2118

WAR DIARY
or
INTELLIGENCE SUMMARY
(Erase heading not required.)

Instructions regarding War Diaries and Intelligence Summaries are contained in F. S. Regs., Part II. and the Staff Manual respectively. Title Pages will be prepared in manuscript.

Place	Date	Hour	Summary of Events and Information	Remarks and references to Appendices
VALHOUN.	22.5.17	8.10 PM	Battalion marched to Billets at ST. HILAIRE. The Secretary of State for War (Lord Derby) inspected the Battalion en route at about 1 PM	
ST. HILAIRE.	" "	4 PM.	Arrived in Billets.	
— " —	23.5.17		Battalion resting for a day.	
— " —	24.5.17	7.45 AM	Battalion marched to Billets at STEENBECQUE (LE BAS).	
STEENBECQUE (LE BAS).	— " —	2.30 PM	Arrived in Billets.	
— " —	25.5.17	7.20 AM	Battalion marched to Billets in CAESTRE area.	
CAESTRE.	— " —	11.30 AM	Arrived in Billets.	
— " —	26.5.17	7.20 AM	Battalion marched to Billets in STEENVOORDE area (South of WATOU).	
STEENVOORDE.	26.5.17	9.40 AM	Arrived in Billets.	
— " —	27.5.17		Battalion resting.	
— " —	28.5.17	6.30 PM	Battalion marched to Huts at BRANDHOEK.	
BRANDHOEK	— " —	10.50 PM	Arrived in Huts.	
— " —	29.5.17	10.15 PM	Battalion entrained for YPRES to relieve 19th Battn. K.L.R. in Support Trenches HOOGE Sector.	
Support Trenches.	30.5.17	3.30 AM	Relief complete.	
— " —	— " —		CASUALTY: 1 O.R. wounded.	
— " —	31.5.17		Battalion in Support Trenches - HOOGE Sector.	

[signature]
LIEUT. COLONEL.
COM.DG. 17th (SERVICE) BATT. THE LIVERPOOL REGT.

Vol 20
89/31

20.C
5 sheets

CONFIDENTIAL.

WAR DIARY.

OF

17TH BN. "THE KING'S" (LIVERPOOL REGIMENT).

From JUNE 1ST 1917. TO JUNE 30TH 1917.

(VOLUME 20.)

20.C
5 sheets

Army Form C. 2118

WAR DIARY or INTELLIGENCE SUMMARY

(Erase heading not required.)

17TH (SERVICE) BATT:
ORDERLY ROOM
2 JULY 1917
THE LIVERPOOL REGT.

Place	Date	Hour	Summary of Events and Information	Remarks and references to Appendices
SUPPORT TRENCHES.	1.6.17		Battalion in Support Trenches, HOOGE Sector. 6 Platoons in YPRES. 2 Companies furnished Working Parties for the Front Line.	
- do -	2.6.17		Battalion in Support Trenches HOOGE Sector. 2 Companies furnished working Parties for the Front Line.	
- do -	3.6.17		Battalion in Support Trenches. Usual Working Parties.	
- do -	4.6.17		Battalion in Support Trenches. Wounded 1 O.R.	
- do -	5.6.17		Battalion in Support Trenches.	
- do -		11.0 PM	Relief commenced by 24th Division and Battalion moved into CAVALRY BARRACKS, YPRES.	
YPRES.	6.6.17		Battalion in CAVALRY BARRACKS, YPRES. (1 Company in INFANTRY BARRACKS) Wounded 1 O.R.	
SUPPORT TRENCHES.		10.0 PM	Battalion commenced to move into SUPPORT TRENCHES, VAN HOOGE Sector. Relieved units of 24th Division, who were moving into Assembly Trenches.	
- do -	7.6.17	1.20 AM	Battalion in Support Trenches. CASUALTIES 5 O.R. Wounded.	
- do -		3.19 AM	Mines were "blown" under HILL 60, and MESSINES RIDGE. (on the Right), and Artillery bombardment commenced.	
- do -		3.10 AM	Divisions on the Right attacked German Front Line System.	
- do -	8.6.17		Battalion in Front & Support Lines. ('B' & 'D' Coys in Front Line).	
- do -		11.30 PM	Relief commenced by 2nd Bn. R.S.F. ('B' & 'D' Battalion left for VLAMERTINGHE, and entrained for POPERINGHE. Detrained at POPERINGHE and marched to Billets in area between POPERINGHE and ABEELE.	
POPERINGHE	9.6.17		Arrived in Billets. ('B' Company remained in Front Line attached to 2nd Bn. Bedfordshire Regt.) Casualties 8/9.6.17. Killed 10 O.R. 15 O.R. Wounded.	
ABEELE		6.30 AM		
- do -	10.6.17		In Billets.	

Army Form C. 2118

WAR DIARY
or
INTELLIGENCE SUMMARY
(Erase heading not required.)

Instructions regarding War Diaries and Intelligence Summaries are contained in F. S. Regs., Part II. and the Staff Manual respectively. Title Pages will be prepared in manuscript.

Place	Date	Hour	Summary of Events and Information	Remarks and references to Appendices
POPERINGHE - ABEELE area	11-6-17		Battalion in Billets. Ordinary Drill and Training carried out.	
- do -	12-6-17		Training - Arm - Squad Drill, Bombing, Bayonet Fighting etc.	
- do -	13-6-17		— do —	
- do -	14-6-17		Ordinary Drill and Training carried out.	
- do -	15-6-17		Bombing, Bayonet Fighting & Signalling Classes. Platoon Instruction.	
- do -	16-6-17		Drill and Training. REINFORCEMENT: 2/Lieuts. R. GILL. F.B. WALKER. E.N. GOLDSPINK. T.H. AVERILL. W.E. WATSON. R.G. SMERDON and 62 Other Ranks arrived.	
- do -	17-6-17		Church Parade. Draft inspected by C.O., and posted to Coys. REINFORCEMENT: 26 Other Ranks.	
- do -	18-6-17		Arm + Squad Drill and nance Instructional Classes.	
- do -	19-6-17		Battalion engaged in Arm - Squad Drill and Sectional Instruction.	
- do -	20-6-17		40 Other Ranks Proceeded to Heavy Artillery as a Working Party.	
- do -	-	4.30 P.M.	Battalion marched from POPERINGHE - ABEELE Area to CANAL RESERVE CAMP. (near DICKEBUSCH). Arrived in Camp - 7.30 P.M.	
CANAL RESERVE CAMP. (DICKEBUSCH).	21-6-17	7.30 P.M.	Battalion in Camp. Sectional Instruction carried out.	
"	22-6-17		Battalion furnished Working Party of 500 Other Ranks to dig Cable Trench near ZILLEBEKE LAKE.	
- do -	23-6-17		Bayonet Fighting + Bombing carried out in afternoon.	
- do -	24-6-17		Battalion furnished Working Party of 500 Other Ranks to dig Cable Trench near ZILLEBEKE LAKE.	

Army Form C. 2118

WAR DIARY
or
INTELLIGENCE SUMMARY
(Erase heading not required.)

Instructions regarding War Diaries and Intelligence Summaries are contained in F.S. Regs., Part II. and the Staff Manual respectively. Title Pages will be prepared in manuscript.

Place	Date	Hour	Summary of Events and Information	Remarks and references to Appendices
CANAL RESERVE CAMP.	25.6.17		Battalion furnished Working Party of 5 Officers + 150 Other Ranks for 2nd Canadian Tunnelling Company. Also Working Party of 50 oR.	
- do -		8 P.M.	REINFORCEMENT. 111 Other Ranks arrived. fixing up Shell holes near ZILLEBEKE LAKE and constructing light Railway.	
- do -	26.6.17		REINFORCEMENT. 35 Other Ranks arrived.	
- do -	27.6.17	3. A.M.	Working Party of 50 oR. (for constructing light Railway near ZILLEBEKE LAKE) furnished by 'D' Company.	
CHATEAU SEGARD.	- do -	8.30 P.M.	Battalion moved up into Support Area at CHATEAU SEGARD.	
	- do -	9.30 P.M.	Arrived in Support area. In Bivouacs & Shelters.	
	28.6.17	9.30 P.M.	Battalion moved into Front line Trenches in OBSERVATORY Ridge. REINFORCEMENT: 2/Lt L.E.L. YORK.	
FRONT LINE TRENCHES.	29.6.17	2.A.M.	Seven to relieve 19th Bn. Manchester Regt. Battn HQ in CRAB CRAWL DUG-OUTS. Relief complete.	
- do -	30.6.17		Battalion in Front line Trenches.	

J.W.Rich. LIEUT. COLONEL
COMdg 17th (SERVICE) BATTn THE LIVERPOOL REGt

CONFIDENTIAL.

WAR DIARY.

OF

17TH BATTALION "THE KING'S" (LIVERPOOL REGIMENT.)

FROM 1ST JULY 1917 TO 31ST JULY 1917.

VOLUME 21.

Army Form C. 2118

WAR DIARY
or
INTELLIGENCE SUMMARY
(Erase heading not required.)

Instructions regarding War Diaries and Intelligence Summaries are contained in F.S. Regs., Part II. and the Staff Manual respectively. Title Pages will be prepared in manuscript.

Place	Date	Hour	Summary of Events and Information	Remarks and references to Appendices
FRONT LINE TRENCHES.	1/7/17.		Battalion holding Front Line - OBSERVATORY RIDGE SECTOR, YPRES.	
- do -	2/7/17.		- do -	
- do -	3/7/17.		REINFORCEMENT: Capt. J.H. JOSEPH reported for duty.	
- do -	4/7/17.	12.15a.m.	Battalion in Front Line Trenches. Lieut. A. CHAVASSE + 8 Other Ranks left our trenches to Patrol German Front Line, with the object of ascertaining disposition of enemy, obtaining identification + killing occupants. This Patrol on nearing enemy wire, encountered a German Patrol, which opened fire on them - wounding Lt. CHAVASSE. Our Patrol withdrew to our lines. Lieut. CHAVASSE was missing and Capt. A.I. DRAPER, Capt. C.E. TORREY, Capt. F.B. CHAVASSE (R.A.M.C.) 2/Lieut. C.A. PETERS, 4/Cpl. H. DIXON (11531) went searched No Mans Land for him. During the search, Capt. C.E. TORREY was wounded and taken in to our trenches. 2/Lt. C.A. PETERS and 4/Cpl. DIXON discovered Lieut. CHAVASSE in a shell hole; 2/Lt. PETERS was killed when returning to our lines for assistance to carry the wounded Officer in. 4/Cpl. DIXON remaining to bandage his wounds. After awaiting the arrival of the necessary assistance, 4/Cpl. DIXON returned for Stretcher Bearers to carry Lt. CHAVASSE in; but, on going back, the party were unable to find the Officer, and had to return on account of the dawn breaking.	
- do -	5/7/17.		Battalion holding Front Line. L/Cpl. DIXON + 3 men left our trenches to search for Lieut. CHAVASSE. Capt. F.B. CHAVASSE also went across No Mans Land to endeavour to find his brother; but the wounded Officer was not discovered. The body of 2/Lieut. C.A. PETERS was carried to our lines, by	

Army Form C. 2118

WAR DIARY
or
INTELLIGENCE SUMMARY
(Erase heading not required.)

Instructions regarding War Diaries and Intelligence Summaries are contained in F.S. Regs., Part II. and the Staff Manual respectively. Title Pages will be prepared in manuscript.

Place	Date	Hour	Summary of Events and Information	Remarks and references to Appendices
FRONT LINE TRENCHES.	6/7/17.		Another quiet day. Lt. Col. T.S. RENDALL arrived to assume command of Battalion.	
- do -	6/7/17.	11 PM.	Battalion was relieved by 7th Battn. "The Buffs" in the Front line, commencing at 11 PM. Relief complete. Battalion marched by Companies to Huts, movements are	
OTTAWA CAMP.	7/7/17.	3 AM.	OTTAWA CAMP arriving at 5 AM.	
		5 AM.	Lt. Col. J.N. PECK. M.C. left for England, and Lt. Col. T.S. RENDALL took over command of Battalion.	
	- " -	11.30 AM.	Battalion marched from OTTAWA CAMP to Entraining Point near BUSSEBOOM.	
BUSSEBOOM. WATTEN.	- " -	2 PM.	Entrained for WATTEN, arriving at 7.45 PM.	
	- " -	8 PM.	Marched to Billets at BLANC PIGNON. (near AUDRUICQ).	
BLANC PIGNON.	- " -	11.15 AM.	Arrived in Billets in BLANC PIGNON area.	
- do -	8/7/17.		Battalion engaged in cleaning up, refitting etc.	
- do -	9/7/17.		Platoon Inspections - Sectional Drill and Training.	
- do -	10/7/17.		Battalion engaged in attack practice on Battalion Parade Ground.	
- do -	11/7/17.		Training - Arm Squad Drill.	
- do -	12/7/17.	9 AM.	Battalion paraded to witness demonstration in mining.	
	- " -	1.15 PM.	Firing practice carried on under Company arrangements. Battalion marched to Brigade Training Ground near NORDAUSQUES to participate in Brigade Practice Attack, returning to Billets at about 7.15 PM.	
- do -	13/7/17.	9 AM.	Parades under Company arrangements from 9 AM. to 11 AM.	
	- " -	12.15 PM.	Battalion marched to GUEMY for Field Firing Practice. On completion of Firing Practice, Battalion bivouaced near TOURNEHEM for the night.	

WAR DIARY
or
INTELLIGENCE SUMMARY
(Erase heading not required.)

Army Form C. 2118

Instructions regarding War Diaries and Intelligence Summaries are contained in F.S. Regs., Part II. and the Staff Manual respectively. Title Pages will be prepared in manuscript.

Place	Date	Hour	Summary of Events and Information	Remarks and references to Appendices
BLANC PIGNON	14/7/17	3.30 AM	Battalion took part in a Divisional Practice Attack, returning to Billets about 9.30 AM	
- do -	15/7/17		Day was devoted to overhaul and repair of Boots and Clothing.	
- do -	16/7/17	8.15 AM	Battalion marched to Training Area near NORDAUSQUES to take part in Divisional Practice Attack to commence at 10.30 AM. Practice in Consolidation of captured positions was carried out.	
- do -	17/7/17	9 AM.	All Companies practised Wiring from 9 AM for one hour each. Bayonet Fighting, Squad and Company Drill in the afternoon.	
- do -	18/7/17	9 AM.	Rifle Grenade Section moved to the QUARRY near NORDAUSQUES to practise firing Grenades. Remaining Sections carried out Sectional Training in the Battalion area. During this period of Training the Commanding Officer held Conferences with Officers & N.C.Os. daily.	
- do -	19/7/17	12.15 PM	Afternoon - Half Holiday. Battalion marched to Entrainment Point near RECQUES and entrained at 2 PM. for STEENVOORDE area.	
	- "-	2 PM.	REINFORCEMENT. - 2/Lt. E. DAVIES arrived	
LE TEMPLE (near STEENVOORDE)	- "-	8 PM.	Detrained at Cross-roads at LE TEMPLE, and proceeded to Billets in that neighbourhood.	
- do -	20/7/17.		Company Training carried out. Commanding Officer's Conference with all Officers and Senior N.C.Os.	
- do -	21/7/17.		Company Parades. Lewis Gun classes were conducted by Sgt. BRYAN (Battn. L.G. Instructor) and Sgt. WILLMOTT. (G.H.Q. School Instructor.)	
- do -	22/7/17.		Church Service.	

WAR DIARY
or
INTELLIGENCE SUMMARY

(Erase heading not required.)

Army Form C. 2118

Place	Date	Hour	Summary of Events and Information	Remarks and references to Appendices
LE TEMPLE. (near STEENVOORDE).	23/7/17.		Company Training and lewis Gun Classes. Commanding Officer's Conference for all Officers and Senior N.C.Os.	
- do -	24/7/17.	6.45AM	Battalion marched from LE TEMPLE to CONNAUGHT CAMP (L. 34. b. - Sheet 27).	
CONNAUGHT CAMP.	- " -	11.25AM	Arrived in Camp.	
- do -	25/7/17.		Training under Company arrangements. Commanding Officer's Conference as usual.	
- do -	26/7/17.		Training under Company arrangements. - Commanding Officer's Conference	
- do -	27/7/17.		- ditto - do -	
- do -	28/7/17.		All Platoons visited the "Picture Bomb". (Plan of German Trenches to be attacked in forthcoming operations). Commanding Officer's Conference. Battalion Paraded for a lecture on "MORALE" Was given by the Commanding Officer.	
- do -	29/7/17.	9.45 AM	Battalion marched to PALACE CAMP. (H. 25. c. 4/6) near OUDERDOM, arriving	
- do -	- " -	7.15PM	at 9.45 PM.	
PALACE CAMP.	- " -	9.45PM		
- do -	29/7/17.		Day devoted to drawing of Ammunition, Grenades, Tools &c. necessary for operations. 229 O.R. (Reserve Personnel) to Corps Reinforcement Camp.	
- do -	- " -	9.30PM	Battalion marched to trenches in CHATEAU SEGARD area.	
CHATEAU SEGARD.	30/7/17.	8.30PM	Battalion moved to PROMENADE Trench on South side of ZILLEBEKE LAKE. No casualties were sustained + Battn. assembled in accordance with orders.	
PROMENADE TRENCH.	31/7/17.	5.15AM	Battalion moved in order "A" "B" "C" "D" Companies to the Forward Assembly	

ns

WAR DIARY
or
INTELLIGENCE SUMMARY
(Erase heading not required.)

Army Form C. 2118

Instructions regarding War Diaries and Intelligence Summaries are contained in F. S. Regs., Part II. and the Staff Manual respectively. Title Pages will be prepared in manuscript.

Place	Date	Hour	Summary of Events and Information	Remarks and references to Appendices
	31/7/17		Position at MAPLE COPSE, where 2/Lieut. N. HENRY. M.C. had made arrangements for marking Position with screw pickets and sandbags. The Battalion came under desultory shell fire at ZILLEBEKE. This increased in severity in the neighbourhood of MAPLE COPSE, and the Regt.Sgt.Major was wounded, Signalling Sergt. J.D.RIGBY killed, also 3 Signallers and a Battalion Runner. Two men out of action. On arrival at Forward Assembly Position, 2/Lieut. C.L. CHILDS (kept Female Guide) was wounded and 2/Lieut C. BASSINGHAM took his place.	
		7.50 AM	BLUE LINE reported captured. Battalion moved forward in artillery formation of half Company columns on a bearing of 104° Magnetic, with orders to halt just West of STIRLING CASTLE. During the advance the Battalion was shelled with Field Guns, 5.9" and 8" Howitzers, and suffered casualties from Machine Gun fire.	
		8.40 AM	On arrival at STIRLING CASTLE at 8.40 AM, it was reported that our troops were held up between BLUE and BLACK lines. Seeing that the Programme of operations was not being carried out to time, and that every minute of delay caused a larger gap between the leading waves and the barrage, the Commanding Officer ordered the Battalion forward with the idea of reinforcing and carrying forward the leading troops into the BLACK line. The information as to the leading troops was erroneous, and on crossing the crest of the STIRLING CASTLE Ridge, it was discovered that no British troops were in front of this Battalion. In spite of the fact that the barrage was some four hours	

1875 Wt. W593/826 1,000,000 4/15 J.B.C. & A. A.D.S.S./Forms/C. 2118.

WAR DIARY
or
INTELLIGENCE SUMMARY
(Erase heading not required.)

Army Form C. 2118

Instructions regarding War Diaries and Intelligence Summaries are contained in F.S. Regs., Part II. and the Staff Manual respectively. Title Pages will be prepared in manuscript.

Place	Date	Hour	Summary of Events and Information	Remarks and references to Appendices
	31/7/17		ahead of the 17th Battn. K.L.R., and in spite of heavy Machine Gun, Rifle and Shell fire, the Battalion pushed on until the left ("C" Company, Capt. G.G. RYLANDS), rested on CLAPHAM JUNCTION. The advance was stopped. — The Battalion dug itself in and held on to the ground gained in spite of very severe shelling from Field Guns and 5.9" Howitzers. During this shelling the following casualties were sustained:— Lieut. F.R. DIMOND (O.C. "B" Coy.) } Killed. 2/Lieut. E.N. GOLDSPINK ("A" Coy.) } 35 Other Ranks Killed. 2/Lieut. C. BASSINGHAM ("D" Coy.) } Wounded. 2/Lieut. L.E.L. YORK ("D" Coy.) } 120 Other Ranks Wounded. (A large proportion of senior N.C.O.s were among the above casualties). *[signed]* Newall LIEUT. COLONEL, 17th (SERVICE) BATT: THE LIVERPOOL REGT.	

CONFIDENTIAL.

WAR DIARY.

OF

17ᵀᴴ BN. "THE KING'S". (LIVERPOOL REGT).

FROM: 1ˢᵀ AUGUST 1917.   TO: 31ˢᵀ AUGUST 1917.

(VOLUME 29.)

Army Form C. 2118

WAR DIARY
or
INTELLIGENCE SUMMARY
(Erase heading not required.)

Instructions regarding War Diaries and Intelligence Summaries are contained in F.S. Regs., Part II. and the Staff Manual respectively. Title Pages will be prepared in manuscript.

Place	Date	Hour	Summary of Events and Information	Remarks and references to Appendices
	1/8/17.		Battalion holding ground gained, and consolidating Front Line - Batn. H.Q. consequently under enemy shell fire.	
	2/8/17.		Battalion consolidating. Enemy shelling whole of day.	
	3/8/17.		— do —	
			The following casualties were sustained during period 1/8/17 - 3/8/17 :-	
			Killed. Capt. J. H. JOSEPH + 17 Other Ranks	
			Wounded. 2/Lt. E. DAVIES + 74 — do —	
			Missing — 12 — do —	
	3/8/17.	10.30 p.m.	Battalion relieved by 7th Royal West Kents. and moved to ZILLEBEKE LAKE, where hot food was provided.	
CHATEAU SEGARD	4/8/17.	6 a.m.	Moved to CHATEAU SEGARD.	
		4 p.m.	Battalion moved by Bus to OTTAWA CAMP near OUDERDOM.	

Army Form C. 2118.

WAR DIARY
or
INTELLIGENCE SUMMARY
(Erase heading not required.)

Instructions regarding War Diaries and Intelligence Summaries are contained in F.S. Regs., Part II. and the Staff Manual respectively. Title Pages will be prepared in manuscript.

Place	Date	Hour	Summary of Events and Information	Remarks and references to Appendices
OTTAWA CAMP.	5/8/17.	12.45 PM.	Battalion marched to OUDERDOM STATION and entrained at 1.15 PM.	
GOEDEWAERSVELDE.	" "	6 PM.	Arrived in Billets at GOEDWAERSVELDE.	
- do -	6/8/17.		Day spent in cleaning equipment, and refitting.	
- do -	7/8/17.	7 AM.	Marched to OUTTERSTEENE.	
OUTTERSTEENE.	" "	10.30 AM.	Arrived in Billets (2 Companies in Tents).	
- do -	8/8/17.		Day spent in Bathing, repairing clothes + refitting equipment.	
- do -	9/8/17.	10 AM.	Battalion proceeded on route march, returning at 12.30 PM.	
- do -	10/8/17.	6.45 PM.	Marched from OUTTERSTEENE to Camp near ST. JANS CAPPEL.	
Camp near ST. JANS CAPPEL.	" "	9.15 PM.	Arrived in Camp. S.I. d.7/6. (Sheet 28D)	
- do -	11/8/17.		Battalion engaged in Sectional Training, Squad Drill, Bayonet Fighting, Musketry etc.	
- do -	12/8/17.		Church Services.	
- do -	13/8/17.	10 AM.	Battalion paraded for inspection by Commanding Officer. Remainder of day spent in Sectional Training.	
- do -	14/8/17.		Sectional Training.	
- do -	" "	2.30 PM.	Battalion paraded for rehearsal for Ceremonial Drill.	
- do -	15/8/17.	1 PM.	Battalion marched to Brigade Parade ground for inspection by General PLUMMER, Commander of Second Army. Sectional Training carried out by all companies, also one hour drill practice in Rapid Winning.	
- do -	16/8/17.	2 PM.	Battalion under Regimental Sgt. Major.	

Army Form C. 2118

WAR DIARY
or
INTELLIGENCE SUMMARY
(Erase heading not required.)

Instructions regarding War Diaries and Intelligence Summaries are contained in F.S. Regs, Part II. and the Staff Manual respectively. Title Pages will be prepared in manuscript.

Place	Date	Hour	Summary of Events and Information	Remarks and references to Appendices
Camp near ST. JANS CAPPELL	17/8/17	7.30AM	"B" Company proceeded to Brigade Training Area (near BOESCHEPE) to dig Practice Trenches.	
	-do-	8 AM	"A" Company carried out Firing Practice on Battalion Range.	
	-do-	9 AM	"C" + "D" Companies engaged in Sectional Training + Gas Helmet Drill. Commanding Officer held Kit Inspections of "C" + "D" Coys.	
-do-	18/8/17	8 AM	During the morning, Firing Practice on Battalion Range. "B" Company carried out Sectional Training + Gas Helmet Drill. Remainder of Battalion engaged in Sectional Training + Gas Helmet Drill. Commanding Officer held Kit Inspection of "A" Coy. + Transport Section.	
	-do-	1 PM.	Battalion proceeded to Brigade Parade Ground for Gas Demonstration, passing through a Gas Cloud wearing Box Respirators.	
-do-	19/8/17		Church Services.	
-do-	20/8/17		This day was observed as a holiday. Brigade Sports were held.	
-do-	21/8/17	7.30AM	"C" + "D" Companies proceeded as Working Party to Brigade Training Area for work on Practice Trenches.	
			"A" + "B" Companies practiced on Battalion Range during day.	
-do-	22/8/17	7.45AM	Battalion marched to Brigade Training Area. Attack Practice on Strong Point carried out by Platoons.	
-do-	23/8/17	7.50AM	Wiring Practice, Sectional Training + Bayonet Fighting carried out. Battalion marched from Camp at 5.1.d 7/6. to Camp at M.35.d 7/9. near DRANOUTRE.	
DRANOUTRE	-do-	9.5 AM	Arrived in Camp.	

Army Form C. 2118

WAR DIARY
or
INTELLIGENCE SUMMARY
(Erase heading not required.)

Instructions regarding War Diaries and Intelligence Summaries are contained in F.S. Regs., Part II. and the Staff Manual respectively. Title Pages will be prepared in manuscript.

Place	Date	Hour	Summary of Events and Information	Remarks and references to Appendices
DRANOUTRE.	24/8/17	10 AM	Battalion paraded for Battalion Drill. Sectional Training + Classes for Instruction in Arms such Bayonet Fighting, and Signalling carried out during day.	
- do -	25/8/17		Companies travelled to Butts during morning. "C" + "D" Companies carried out Firing Practice on range. Remainder of Battalion engaged in Sectional Training, Instructional Classes and Company Kit Inspections.	
- do -	26/8/17		Church Service. Battalion Shooting Competition held on Rifle Range. Conditions as for 15 Rounds Rapid Practice.	
- do -	27/8/17	7.30 AM	Battalion marched to Brigade Training Area. for Wiring + Consolidation Practice.	
- do -	28/8/17		Battalion engaged in Physical Drill. Bayonet Fighting, Musketry, Gas Helmet Drill + Sectional Training. Bombers + Rifle Grenadiers moved to Bombing Pits for Practice with inspective Instructors.	
- do -	29/8/17	2 PM	Classes under respective Instructors. Battalion marched to Camp at MM N. 28. b. 3/2. (Reserve Area).	
Camp at N.28.b.3/2.	-"-	8.10 PM	Arrived in Camp.	
- do -	30/8/17		Companies engaged on Working Parties in Front Line System.	
- do -	31/8/17		Working Parties provided for Front Line. CASUALTIES 30/8/17. 1 Sgt. JOHNSON Killed. 1 O.R. Wounded.	

W. Russell .... LIEUT. COLONEL
COMDG 17TH (SERVICE) BATT: THE LIVERPOOL REGT

CONFIDENTIAL.

WAR DIARY.

OF

17TH BN. "THE KING'S" (LIVERPOOL REGT).

From: 1-9-1917. To: 30-9-1917.

(VOLUME XXIII).

Army Form C. 2118

WAR DIARY
or
INTELLIGENCE SUMMARY

(Erase heading not required.)

Instructions regarding War Diaries and Intelligence Summaries are contained in F. S. Regs., Part II. and the Staff Manual respectively. Title Pages will be prepared in manuscript.

Place	Date	Hour	Summary of Events and Information	Remarks and references to Appendices
Camp at N.28.b. 8/2.	1.9.17		Battalion engaged on Working Parties.	
- do -	2.9.17		Companies marched to Brigade Baths at LINDENHOEK. Divine Services.	
- do -	- " -	8 P.M.	Battalion marched to Support Area, and relieved 19th Battn. K.L.R.	
Support (RIGHT BATTALION HOLLEBEKE SECTOR)	- " -	10 P.M.	Relief complete.	
- do -	3.9.17		Battalion in Support. 1 O.R. Wounded.	
- do -	4.9.17	9.30 pm	Following moves took place on relief by 20th Bn. K.L.R. :- "B" Coy. to DAMM STRASSE. "B" Coy. to DENYS FARM. "D" Coy. to ENGLEBRIE Fm. Battn. H.Q. to DAMM STRASSE. Battalion in position as Right Support Battalion.	
- do -	- " -	10.45 pm	Move complete. REINFORCEMENT: 2/Lieuts. J.S.REA. C.R. TAYLOR. and J. HODGSON. HOLLEBEKE Sector.	
- do -	5.9.17		Battalion in Support. Working & Carrying Parties provided for Front Line. MAJOR S.H. CHAPIN. D.S.O. transferred to 24th I.B.D. for "sick". MAJOR A.I. DRAPER took over duties of Second-in-Command.	
- do -	- " -		Battn. H.Q. moved from DAMM STRASSE to H.Q. in DENYS WOOD vacated by 19th Battn. K.L.R. "B" & "C" Coy. moved to DAMM STRASSE. Capt. F.B. CHAVASSE. M.C. (R.A.M.C.) left for No. 11. C.C.S. - Replaced by Capt. W.G.L. WAMBEEK(RAMC)	
- do -	6.9.17	4.30 P.M.	Battalion in Support. 13 other ranks to Hospital "Gassed".	
- do -	7.9.17		Battalion in Support.	
- do -	8.9.17		Battalion relieved 19th Battn. K.L.R. in Front Line System. REINFORCEMENT: 2/Lieut. F.A. GIBSON. and 2/Lieut. H. GOODIER.	
FRONT LINE. HOLLEBEKE Sector.	9.9.17	9 P.M.	Battalion in Front Line. 3 Posts. taken over from 2nd Bn. Bedfordshire Regt. 1 O.R. Wounded.	
- do -	10.9.17			
- do -	11.9.17		Disposition in the Line re-organised - 3 Coys. in Front Line ("C" "A" "D"). 1 Coy. in Support at ROSEWOOD (B)	

1875 Wt. W593/826 1,000,000 4/15 J.B.C. & A. A.D.S.S./Forms/C.2118.

Army Form C. 2118

WAR DIARY
or
INTELLIGENCE SUMMARY
(Erase heading not required.)

Instructions regarding War Diaries and Intelligence Summaries are contained in F. S. Regs., Part II. and the Staff Manual respectively. Title Pages will be prepared in manuscript.

Place	Date	Hour	Summary of Events and Information	Remarks and references to Appendices
FRONT LINE. HOLLEBEKE Sector	12.9.17		Battalion in Front and Shell Hole Line.	
- do -	13.9.17		Battalion holding Front Line. Wiring Parties putting out trenching wire.	
- do -	14.9.17		REINFORCEMENT: 7/him. J. H. BURROWS.	
- do -	15.9.17	8 A.M.	Holding Front Line. Enemies engaged on usual Trench Working Parties. Prisoners rations from Shell Hole line, leaving Camp Sector only. Our Artillery put up a Practice Barrage with guns of all calibre in enemies lines. Duration of Barrage - half an hour. 1 O.R. wounded (Accidentally).	
- do -	16.9.17	10 A.M.	Our Artillery put up a Second Practice Barrage on enemies lines, lasting 30 minutes. Enemy replied with a light Barrage on our Front and Support line. CASUALTIES: 1 Officer, 2 I.O.R. killed - 1 O.R. wounded.	
- do -		4 P.M.	Third Practice Barrage, of 30 minutes duration.	
- do -	16.17.9.17		Patrol, lead by Cpl. W. JACKSON (12364). discovered a large enemy Working Party (about 50 strong) in front of German Front Line, and information was sent to Artillery, which put up a concentrated barrage. Lewis Guns & Trench Mortars co-operated on each flank of the barrage. It is believed the enemy sustained a number of casualties.	Enemy replied which usual strafe on French line Diploma
- do -	17.9.17.	8 A.M.	French Practice Barrage put up on enemy's lines - ditto	
- do -	- " -	5 P.M.	Patrol, lead by Cpl. L. TAYLOR. (49041). discovered a large party of Germans working in front of WH 122 FARM. Artillery immediately put up a concentrated barrage. Machine Guns and Trench Mortars co. operated on either flank of barrage. This operation was also an entire success.	

Army Form C. 2118

WAR DIARY
or
INTELLIGENCE SUMMARY
(Erase heading not required.)

Instructions regarding War Diaries and Intelligence Summaries are contained in F.S. Regs., Part II. and the Staff Manual respectively. Title Pages will be prepared in manuscript.

Place	Date	Hour	Summary of Events and Information	Remarks and references to Appendices
FRONT LINE.	18/9/17	6 AM.	Sixth Practice Barrage put over. Enemy replied in usual.	
			CASUALTIES: 1 OR Killed, 1 OR Wounded.	
	-"-	Noon.	Seventh Practice Barrage. -do- 45 minutes Duration. Enemy replied	
	-"-	8.30PM	Eighth -do- -do- slightly heavier Barrage than before.	
-do-	19/9/17	5 AM.	Ninth Practice Barrage.	
		3.30AM	Tenth -do-	
		10.55PM	Battalion relieved by 19th Batt. K.L.R. and moved to Support Trenches, HQ. in DENYS WOOD.	
SUPPORT AREA	20/9/17	5.40AM	ZERO for Second + Fifth Army attack on the left.	
	-"-	9 PM	Battalion relieved by 16th Bn. Manchester Regiment. Marched from Support Positions to PARRAIN FARM CAMP, N 28 b. 7/9 (Sheet 28).	
PARRAIN FARM	-"-	11.45PM	Move complete.	
-do-	21/9/17		REINFORCEMENT: 35 Other Ranks.	
			Day Spent in refitting + cleaning equipment.	
	-"-	7.30AM	"A" Company proceeded to LINDEN HOEK for Shutting. Baths. LINDEN HOEK.	
-do-	22/9/17		"A", "B", "C", H.Q. Companies – Bathing at Brigade Baths. LINDEN HOEK.	
	-"-		Remainder of day spent in cleaning equipment.	
-do-	23/9/17		Church Services. – Working Parties provided.	
-do-	24/9/17	9 AM to 12 Noon	All Companies instructed in the use of German Grenades. (2 Boxes wire salved during the day in trenches).of	
	-"-	2.30 – 4 PM	Divisional Trench Order read out to Platoons by respective Commanders.	
			REINFORCEMENT: 22 Other Ranks.	
-do-	25/9/17	7.10 AM	"A" Coy. inspected by Commanding Officer. All Companies carried on Platoon Training – Physical Drill + Bayonet Fighting, Bombing +c. Las Winter Drill	

1875 Wt. W593/826 1,000,000 4/15 J.B.C. & A. A.D.S.S./Forms/C. 2118.

Army Form C. 2118

WAR DIARY
or
INTELLIGENCE SUMMARY
(Erase heading not required.)

Instructions regarding War Diaries and Intelligence Summaries are contained in F.S. Regs., Part II. and the Staff Manual respectively. Title Pages will be prepared in manuscript.

Place	Date	Hour	Summary of Events and Information	Remarks and references to Appendices
PARRAIN FARM.	26/9/17	10 AM	"D" Coy. inspected by Commanding Officer.	
- do -	27/9/17		All Companies carried out ½ Bayonet Fighting, Physical Drill, Arm & Squad Drill, Sectional Instruction during morning.	
- '' -		2 P.M.	"B" Coy. inspected by Commanding Officer. All Companies attended a short demonstration of Enemy keeps by Divisional Eng N.C.O. "A", "C", "D" Coys provided Working Parties for the R.E. at night during the day.	
- do -	28/9/17		"B", "C", & "D" Coys. carried out Attack Practice during the day. "A" Company - Revetting Practice.	
- do -	29/9/17	9 & 10 AM	"B" Coy - Close Order Drill. "A", "C", "D" - Attack Practice.	
		11 AM	Battalion paraded, and carried out Battn. Attack Practice. Inter-Company Football matches played during afternoon. Working Parties provided for the R.E. at night.	
- do -	30/9/17		CHURCH SERVICES.	
			INSTRUCTIONAL CLASSES. Lewis Gun & Signalling Classes were held daily during period 22/9/17 - 30/9/17.	

W. Rudall.
LIEUT. COLONEL.
COMDG. 17th (SERVICE BATT.) THE LIVERPOOL REGT.

CONFIDENTIAL.

WAR DIARY.

OF

17ᵀᴴ BATTALION "THE KING'S" (LIVERPOOL REGIMENT.)

FROM 1ˢᵀ OCTOBER 1917. TO 31ˢᵀ OCTOBER 1917.

VOLUME 24.

WAR DIARY
or
INTELLIGENCE SUMMARY
(Erase heading not required.)

Army Form C. 2118

Instructions regarding War Diaries and Intelligence Summaries are contained in F.S. Regs., Part II. and the Staff Manual respectively. Title Pages will be prepared in manuscript.

Place	Date	Hour	Summary of Events and Information	Remarks and references to Appendices
PARRAIN FARM CAMP	1/x/17		Battalion in Camp. Brigade Reserve Area. "B" Company - Revetting practice. "A" and "D" Companies engaged on working parties at night in the line.	
"	2/x/17		"D" Company - Revetting practice. "A" Company - Building rifle range - "C" and "B" Companies engaged on working parties in the line at night.	
"	3/x/17		Revetting practice etc and working parties in the line at night. CONGRATULATORY MESSAGE. The following letter has been received from Divnl. H.Q. "The G.O.C. congratulates the 17th Bn. "The Kings" (Liverpool Regiment) on being the healthiest Battalion in the Division during the past month" (30 Divn A/5033 d/2/10/17) "This reflects great credit on all concerned."	
"	4/x/17		The Battalion used Baths at KEMMEL. 2nd Lt. W.E.WATSON appointed Intelligence Officer vice Lieut H.F.A.PULMAN appointed Assistant Adjutant. CASUALTIES. 2. O.R. wounded. REINFORCEMENT. 8 O.R.	
"	5/x/17		Battalion training in close order drill and Attack and Skirmishing practice. "C" and "D" Companies provided usual working parties at night.	
"	6/x/17		Battalion football match v. 17th Bn. Manchester Regiment - Result Liverpools 5. Manchesters 2. Usual working parties at night.	
"	7/x/17		Divine Services. REINFORCEMENT. 48 O.R. from 18th Bn. K.L.R.	
"	8/x/17		Battalion training in close order drill. Revetting practice. Bayonet fighting etc. Working parties provided at night.	
"	9/x/17		Camp fatigues and Salvage work carried out. Working parties at night.	
"	10/x/17		Football match v. 112th Bn. South Lancs. Regt. Result: South Lancs 2. P'pool. 1. Camp fatigues etc and usual Company training. CASUALTY. 1 O.R.	

WAR DIARY
or
INTELLIGENCE SUMMARY
(Erase heading not required.)

Army Form C. 2118

Instructions regarding War Diaries and Intelligence Summaries are contained in F.S. Regs., Part II. and the Staff Manual respectively. Title Pages will be prepared in manuscript.

Place	Date	Hour	Summary of Events and Information	Remarks and references to Appendices
PARRAIN FARM CAMP	11/4/17	4 P.M.	Battalion marched to relieve 20th Bn. K.L.R. in Support Area HOLLEBEKE sector	
SUPPORT AREA HOLLEBEKE SECTOR	—	8 P.M.	Relief completed – "A" Company in position ENGLEBRIEN FARM. "B" Company RAVINE – "C" Company ROSE WOOD – "D" Company WHITE CHATEAU – and H.Q. in DENYS WOOD.	
—	12/4/17		Battalion in Support Positions. Working and carrying parties provided under R.E. supervision.	
—	13/4/17		Battalion in Support positions. Working and carrying parties provided.	
—	14/4/17		do — do —	
—	15/4/17		MAJOR CAMPBELL N. WATSON. D.S.O. (20th Bn. K.L.R.) assumed (temporary) command of the Battalion vice — — — CASUALTY. 1 O.R. wounded.	
—	16/4/17		LIEUT. COL. T.S. RENDALL. to England. Battalion in Support positions. Working and carrying parties provided. Battalion relieved in Support positions by 2nd Bn. Bedfordshire Regiment on completion of which Battalion marched to relief of 20th Bn. K.L.R. in Front Line positions.	
FRONT LINE HOLLEBEKE SECTOR	—	P.M. 8.15 P.M. No 30	Relief complete – "D" Company LEFT (Shellhole) SECTOR. "B" Company RIGHT (Freehole) sector. "C" Company in Support (OAK SUPPORT TRENCH) "A" Company in reserve – RAVINE and Battn. HQ in RAVINE. CASUALTIES 1 O.R. killed and 1 O.R. wounded.	
—	17/4/17		Battalion holding Front Line positions. Usual works under O.C. Coys. improving positions. Patrols at night. CASUALTIES. 3 O.R. wounded.	
—	18/4/17		Battalion holding Front Line positions – works – sandbagging and baling OAK SUPPORT TRENCH, and wiring Front Line. CASUALTIES. 3 O.R. wounded.	
—	19/4/17		Battalion holding Front Line positions. Usual works & patrols at night. CASUALTY. 1 O.R. wounded.	

WAR DIARY
or
INTELLIGENCE SUMMARY

(Erase heading not required.)

Army Form C. 2118

Place	Date	Hour	Summary of Events and Information	Remarks and references to Appendices
FRONT LINE HOLLEBEKE SECTOR	20/4/17	P.M.	Battalion in front line positions. Work - boring and revetting. Patrols at night.	
"	21/4/17	8.30	Battalion relieved by 2nd Bn. Bedfordshire Regt. and marched independently to PARRAIN FARM CAMP. Arrived in Camp 10.30 P.M. CASUALTIES Major A.I. DRAPER killed and 3 O.R. wounded.	
PARRAIN FARM CAMP	22/4/17		Morning: Cleaning up. Afternoon. Inspection by Commanding Officer.	
"	23/4/17		Battalion bathed at Brigade Baths LINDENHOEK. FUNERAL. A large number of Officers and O.R. attended the funeral of Major A.I. DRAPER at KEMMEL Cemetery at 2.30 P.M.	
"	24/4/17		Morning. Work improving Camp and general training by Companies. Afternoon. Inter-Company football match.	
"	25/4/17		Camp improvement work was again carried out, and Company training in Bullet & Bayonet Fighting, Musketry, etc Machine & Lewis Gun Officers v. Men. Football Match.	
"	26/4/17		Work on Camp and Company training.	
"	27/4/17	1 P.M.	Commanding Officer's Inspection by Companies. Afternoon. Football match. Camp inspected by VIII Corps Commander, who congratulated Battalion on its Smartness.	
"	28/4/17		SPECIAL TASK. The Battalion was allotted a special service. Task of burying a cable 6' deep from cable head at O.15.d 15/80 to meet the duck board track about O.19.d 18/25 and thence along track to Support Battalion H.Q. in DENYS WOOD, a total length of 480 yards. The work was duly accomplished by "A" & "B" Companies the first 240 yards on the night 27/28th and "C" & "D" Companies the remainder on the night 28/29th.	

Army Form C. 2118

WAR DIARY
or
INTELLIGENCE SUMMARY
(Erase heading not required.)

Instructions regarding War Diaries and Intelligence Summaries are contained in F.S. Regs., Part II. and the Staff Manual respectively. Title Pages will be prepared in manuscript.

Place	Date	Hour	Summary of Events and Information	Remarks and references to Appendices
PARRAIN FARM CAMP	29/x/17	9 a.m.	Battalion commenced to move from PARRAIN FARM CAMP to RAMILLIES CAMP at N.27.8.1.6. The 2nd Bn Wilts. Regiment taking over the former camp.	
RAMILLIES CAMP	— —	12 NOON P.M.	Move Completed.	
	— —	3.30	Ceremonial parade at which Medal Ribands for following decorations were presented by Lieut. Gen. SIR AYLMER HUNTER-WESTON, K.C.B., D.S.O., Comdg VIIIth Corps:- MAJOR CAMPBELL N WATSON. Distinguished Service Order. 16109 SGT. NOAH. W.J. 24905 SGT. JONES T. 41916 PTE. SMITH H.E. 15956 SGT. KERR T.G. } Bar to Military Medal Congratulatory messages of appreciation were received on the excellent way in which the parade was carried out and both the Corps & Divisional Commanders spoke in terms of highest praise. The Company lines were inspected by Commanding Officer during the morning. Bathing - A.B. and H.Q. Companies bathed at LINDENHOEK baths "C" and "D" Companies bathed at LINDENHOEK baths during morning.	
— —	30/x/17			
— —	31/x/17	P.M. 3.30	Battalion marched by Companies from RAMILLIES CAMP to relieve the 20th Bn K.L.R. in the Support Area.	
SUPPORT AREA HOLLEBEKE SECTOR	— —	6.30 P.M.	Relief Completed. "A" Company to BOW DUG OUTS - "B" Coy. ENGLEBRIEN FARM - "C" Coy to ROSE WOOD - "D" Coy to GOUDEZEUNE FARM at BN H.Q. in DENNY WOOD	

Campbell N Watson MAJOR
COMMDG 17th (SERVICE) BATTN. THE LIVERPOOL REGT.

Vol 25

25 C
6 sheets

CONFIDENTIAL.

WAR DIARY

OF

17TH BN. "THE KING'S" (LIVERPOOL REGT.)

FROM: 1ST NOVEMBER 1917   TO: 30TH NOVEMBER 1917

(VOLUME 25)

Army Form C. 2118

WAR DIARY
or
INTELLIGENCE SUMMARY
(Erase heading not required.)

Instructions regarding War Diaries and Intelligence Summaries are contained in F.S. Regs., Part II. and the Staff Manual respectively. Title Pages will be prepared in manuscript.

Place	Date	Hour	Summary of Events and Information	Remarks and references to Appendices
SUPPORT AREA HOLLEBEKE SECTOR.	1/11/17		Battalion in Support to Front Line. Capt. W.H. PIERCE. Transferred to ENGLAND — on Duty. REINFORCEMENT from 2/Lieut. A.E. EALING. 13th (L.H.) Bn. K.L.R. - Capt. A.C. MORRELL. 2/Lieut. F.W.	
- do -	2/11/17		THOMAS and 2/Lieut A.E. EALING. REINFORCEMENT. Major J.P. PITTS arrived Battalion in Support from 2nd Bn. Bedfordshire Regt. to assume duties of Second in Command.	
- do -	3/11/17		REINFORCEMENT. 6 Officers arrived from Base. Battalion in Support. 2/Lieuts. E.N. AIERS. J.B. FRIEND. E. JONES. A.H. ELLIS. E.D. FORTE. and P.E. HEMMING. One Officer of U.S.A. Army attached for instruction. 2/Lieut. N.B. DICKINSON. joined Battalion.	
- do -	4/11/17		Battalion in Support. 1 O.R. Wounded. (died later).	
- do -	5/11/17		Battalion in Support. 1 O.R. Wounded. (died later).	
- do -	- " -	9 pm.	Battalion relieved 20th Battn. K.L.R. in the Front Line.	
FRONT LINE HOLLEBEKE SECTOR.	6/11/17		Battalion holding the Front Line. REINFORCEMENT 2/Lt. B.J. FEATHER.	
- do -	7/11/17		- ditto - CASUALTIES. 4 O.R. Killed + 3 Wounded.	
- do -	8/11/17		- ditto - CASUALTY. 1 O.R. Killed & wounded.	
- do -	9/11/17		- ditto - REINFORCEMENT. 2/Lt. J.R. WHITTLE.	
- do -	- " -	1.30 am.	A German was taken prisoner. He belonged to the 2nd Battalion of 153rd Infantry Regt.	
- do -	10/11/17		Battalion holding Front Line.	

WAR DIARY or INTELLIGENCE SUMMARY

Army Form C. 2118

(Erase heading not required.)

Place	Date	Hour	Summary of Events and Information	Remarks and references to Appendices
FRONT LINE HOLLEBEKE SECTOR.	10/11/17	12.30 a.m.	An enemy party, 15 strong, attempted to raid our post at O.6.B.6/4. The enemy raked the post, throwing bombs. A few got in but were ejected after a sharp hand to hand fight. During the encounter the leader of the enemy party (A Sergeant Major) was "taken on" by 5q264 L/Cpl. LIMB J.H. (C Coy). After a struggle the German was mortally wounded, and shortly afterwards L/Cpl. LIMB was mortally wounded, dying shortly afterwards in our post. Our casualties were — L/Cpl. LIMB. and one man wounded. The stranger of our post was 1 N.C.O. and 6 men. NOTE:- L/Cpl. LIMB was awarded the Military Medal by the Corps Commander for his gallantry and good example during the fight with the enemy's party. Battalion relieved by 11th Bn Royal North Lancs Regt. and 2nd Bn Bedfordshire Regt. and marched to RAMILLIES CAMP.	
— do —	10/11/17	8.30 p.m.	Arrived in RAMILLIES CAMP.	
— do —	12/11/17	11.30 p.m.	Day spent in cleaning up, Bathing etc.	
— do —	13/11/17	10 a.m.	Battalion relieving by 60th Australian Infantry Battalion and marched to WAKEFIELD HUTS near LOCRE.	
WAKEFIELD HUTS.	—	12.45 p.m.	Arrived in Camp.	
— do —	14/11/17	—	Companies carried out Arms, Squad & Company Drill during the morning. Commanding Officers Parade in the ——— afternoon. Drill + steel helmet	

Army Form C. 2118

WAR DIARY
or
INTELLIGENCE SUMMARY
(Erase heading not required.)

Instructions regarding War Diaries and Intelligence Summaries are contained in F.S. Regs., Part II. and the Staff Manual respectively. Title Pages will be prepared in manuscript.

Place	Date	Hour	Summary of Events and Information	Remarks and references to Appendices
WAKEFIELD HUTS. LOCRE.	15/11/17		Physical Drill, Bayonet Fighting, Musketry, Arm, Squad & Company Drill carried out by Companies. Afternoon — Inter-Company Football Matches.	
- do -	16/11/17	8.30am.	Battalion moved to STEENVOORDE Area by Bus.	
STEENVOORDE.	-"-	12.45 pm.	Arrived in Billets.	
- do -	17/11/17		Company Training carried out.	
- do -	18/11/17		Church Parades.	
- do -	19/11/17		Company Drill, Rapid Loading Practice, Arm Drill, Bayonet Fighting Physical Drill during the morning. Usual Training carried out during afternoon.	
- do -	20/11/17		—do— Inter-Company Football in afternoon.	
- do -	21/11/17		—	
- do -	22/11/17		Battalion proceeded on Route March in the morning. Adjutants Parade in the afternoon.	
- do -	23/11/17		Companies Practised firing on Rifle Range.	
- do -	24/11/17		Battalion Route March during the morning. Inter-Company Football Matches in the afternoon.	
- do -	25/11/17		Church Parades.	

Army Form C. 2118

WAR DIARY
or
INTELLIGENCE SUMMARY
(Erase heading not required.)

Instructions regarding War Diaries and Intelligence Summaries are contained in F.S. Regs., Part II. and the Staff Manual respectively. Title Pages will be prepared in manuscript.

Place	Date	Hour	Summary of Events and Information	Remarks and references to Appendices
STEENVOORDE.	26/11/17		Battalion carried out firing practice on Rifle Range.	
- do -	27/11/17	8.30 am	Battalion marched to CHIPPEWA CAMP.	
CHIPPEWA CAMP.	- " -	1-30 P.M.	Arrived in Camp.	
- do -	28/11/17		General Cleaning up. Kit Inspections etc. Commanding Officer inspected the Battalion.	
- do -	- " -	2 P.M.	Company Drill etc. carried out. Inter Company Football Matches.	
- do -	29/11/17		Battalion carried out Rifle Range Practice	
- do -	30/11/17		Company Drill, Bayonet Fighting, Musketry in afternoon.	

[signature]
for LIEUT. COLONEL
COMDG. 17TH (SERVICE) BATT. THE LIVERPOOL REGT

1875 Wt. W593/826 1,000,000 4/15 J.B.C. & A. A.D.S.S./Forms/C. 2118.

CONFIDENTIAL.

WAR DIARY

OF

17TH BN "THE KING'S" (LIVERPOOL REGIMENT.)

FROM 1st DECEMBER 1917 TO 31st DECEMBER 1917

VOLUME 26.

Army Form C. 2118

WAR DIARY
or
INTELLIGENCE SUMMARY
(Erase heading not required.)

Instructions regarding War Diaries and Intelligence Summaries are contained in F.S. Regs., Part II. and the Staff Manual respectively. Title Pages will be prepared in manuscript.

Place	Date	Hour	Summary of Events and Information	Remarks and references to Appendices
CHIPPAWA CAMP.	1/12/17		Battalion in huts CHIPPAWA CAMP. Physical Drill, Squad and Company Drill, Musketry etc. - Afternoon - Football match v. 2nd Bn. Beds. Regt.	
"	2/12/17	P.M. 2.0	Divine Services - Afternoon - Football match v. 89th Infy. Bde. and Officers 17th K.L.R. v. Officers 2nd Bn. Beds. Regt.	
"	3/12/17		Battalion entrained at G.35.a.4.0. and detrained at MANOR FARM HALT whence marched to relieve the 17th Bn. Manchester Regt. in POLDERHOEK SECTOR (CENTRE SUB SECTOR) Relief complete. CASUALTIES. Killed 2 OR. Wounded 6 OR.	
FRONT LINE POLDERHOEK SECTOR	4/12/17		Battalion in Front Line - Work on wiring, and revetting PERTH AVENUE. Patrols sent out at night for identification of enemy in front, etc. CASUALTIES. Killed 2 OR. Wounded 4 OR.	
"	5/12/17		Battalion in Front Line - Trench improvement and patrolling. CASUALTIES Wounded 3 OR.	
"	6/12/17		Battalion in Front Line - Captured 2 Bosch prisoners and despatched them to Brigade H.Q. STIRLING CASTLE under escort.	
"	7/12/17		Battalion relieved in POLDERHOEK SECTOR by the 20th Bn. K.L.R. and marched into support at TORR TOP TUNNEL.	
TORR TOP TUNNEL	8/12/17	A.M. 12.30	Battalion arrived in TORR TOP TUNNEL. No casualties. Working and carrying parties provided at night. CASUALTIES Killed 1 OR. Wounded 1 OR.	
"	9/12/17		Battalion in support. Work - making connecting wire and carrying parties supplied.	
"	10/12/17		— do —	
"	11/12/17		— do —	
"	12/12/17		— do —	
"	13/12/17	P.M. 4.0	Battalion relieved in TORR TOP TUNNEL by the 2nd Bn. Royal Scots Fusiliers. Relief complete and Battn. marched to huts in Scottish Wood camp - arriving 5 P.M.	

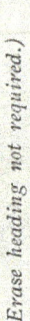

1875. Wt. W593/826 1,000,000 4/15 J.B.C. & A. A.D.S.S./Forms/C. 2118.

Army Form C. 2118

Instructions regarding War Diaries and Intelligence Summaries are contained in F. S. Regs., Part II. and the Staff Manual respectively. Title Pages will be prepared in manuscript.

WAR DIARY
or
INTELLIGENCE SUMMARY

(Erase heading not required.)

Place	Date	Hour	Summary of Events and Information	Remarks and references to Appendices
SCOTTISH WOOD CAMP.	13/12/17		Battalion in Camp. Bathing at BRASSERIE (N.5. F.7.2.) and cleaning up	
"	14/12/17	p.m.	— do — Company inspections, repair and renewal of boots, clothing etc.	
"	—	7.10	Battalion summoned to support of POLDERHOEK SECTOR and marched to TORR TOP TUNNEL at 7.45 P.M. — Arrived 10.35 P.M. — No casualties.	
TORR TOP TUNNEL.	15/12/17		Battalion in support. Carrying parties supplied at night. CASUALTIES — Killed 1 O.R. Wounded 3 O.R.	
"	16/12/17	p.m. 3.0	Battalion relieved in TORR TOP TUNNEL by the 2nd Bn Bedfords Regt and marched to reserve area at SCOTTISH WOOD CAMP, arriving 6 P.M.	
SCOTTISH WOOD CAMP.	17/12/17		Battalion in Camp. Cleaning. Company inspections. Sectional instruction. Afternoon football match V 20th Bn. K.L.R.	
"	18/12/17		Battalion marched from SCOTTISH WOOD to relieve Companies of 16th and 17th Bns Manchester Regiment in the POLDERHOEK SECTOR (CENTRE SUB SECTOR)	
POLDERHOEK SECTOR.	—	p.m. 8.45	Relief complete. No casualties	
"	19/12/17		Battalion holding front line. Heavy gas shell bombardment of the whole sector, between 8 P.M. and 10 P.M. and intermittently during the night necessitating the use of respirators.	
"	20/12/17		Battalion holding front line. 2nd Lieut R GILL M.C, M.M reported enemy in large numbers creeping towards our line about 11.45 A.M. - Rifle and Lewis gun fire failed to disperse them and in reply to our S.O.S. call, an artillery barrage was put down. The enemy scattered and at 12.20 P.M all was quiet. CASUALTIES 2 O.R. Killed.	
"	21/12/17		Battalion relieved in the POLDERHOEK SECTOR by the 20th Bn K.L.R and moved to support positions relieving 18th Bn K.L.R. - "C" and "B" Coys to BODMIN COPSE "A" Company to C.F.A.H.&M. JUNCTION. "D" and "H.Q." Coys to STIRLING CASTLE.	

Army Form C. 2118

WAR DIARY
or
INTELLIGENCE SUMMARY
(Erase heading not required.)

Instructions regarding War Diaries and Intelligence Summaries are contained in F.S. Regs., Part II and the Staff Manual respectively. Title Pages will be prepared in manuscript.

Place	Date	Hour	Summary of Events and Information	Remarks and references to Appendices
Support Sector STIRLING CASTLE.	22/12/17		Battalion in Support. 2 Platoons of "C" Company garrison strong points at J20 c 8 6 and J20 d 9 8. - Usual carrying parties provided.	
"	23/12/17		Battalion in Support — do —	
"	24/12/17		Battalion relieved in support position by 16th Bn. Manchester Regt. and moved by march route to Huts in CHIPPAWA CAMP, arriving at 10 P.M.	
CHIPPAWA CAMP	25/12/17		Battalion in Camp. Christmas day holiday. Divine services and carol service. Special Officers' Dinner.	
"	26/12/17		— do — Holiday. Football match v. 18th Bn. K.L.R. Special dinner to the men and concert in the Church Army Hut.	
"	27/12/17		Battalion in Camp. One hour's Physical Drill — remainder of day Holiday. Football matches. Inter. Coy. Officers' match and Bn. team v. 19th Bn. K.L.R.	
"	28/12/17		Battalion in Camp. One hour Physical Drill. Cleaning and Company inspection.	
"	29/12/17		— do — Divine services.	
"	30/12/17		One hour Physical Drill.	
"			Battalion entrained at FUZEVILLE at 2.30 P.M. and after detraining at MANOR FARM HALT, marched to relief of 18th Bn. Manchester Regt. at POLDERHOEK SECTOR (RIGHT SUB-SECTOR.) No casualties.	
Front Line POLDERHOEK SECTOR.	31/12/17		Battalion holding front line —	

Ronald W Shore Baker
LIEUT. COLONEL
COMDG. 17TH (SERVICE) BATT. LIVERPOOL REGT

CONFIDENTIAL.

WAR DIARY

OF

17TH (SERVICE) BATTN. "THE KING'S" (LIVERPOOL REGT).

FROM 1ST JANUARY 1918 TO 31ST JANUARY 1918.

(VOLUME 27.):

Army Form C. 2118.

WAR DIARY
or
INTELLIGENCE SUMMARY.
(Erase heading not required.)

Instructions regarding War Diaries and Intelligence Summaries are contained in F.S. Regs., Part II. and the Staff Manual respectively. Title pages will be prepared in manuscript.

Stamp: 17TH (SERVICE) BATT: ORDERLY ROOM 3 FEB 1918 THE LIVERPOOL REGT

Place	Date	Hour	Summary of Events and Information	Remarks and references to Appendices
FRONT LINE HOLDER MOEN SECTOR	1/1/18		Battalion holding Front line (RIGHT SUB SECTOR) Patrolling at night and several improvements in trench system carried out. During a heavy bombardment on Battalion's right 2 Boche were seen walking along the MENIN ROAD. They were confirmed and escorted to Brigade H.Q.	
— do —	2/1/18		Battalion relieved by 20th Bn K.R.R. and marched to TORR TOP TUNNEL	
TORR TOP TUNNEL	3/1/18		Battalion in TORR TOP TUNNEL — Working and carrying parties	
— do —	4/1/18		Battalion in Support — Working and carrying parties provided	
— do —	5/1/18		— do —	
— do —	6/1/18	6.30 P.M.	Battalion relieved in TORR TOP TUNNEL by 6th Batt. 3rd S.L.I. (60th Infy Bde) and marched to SWAN CHATEAU arriving 9 P.M.	
SWAN CHATEAU	7/1/18	8 A.M.	— do —	
— do —	7/1/18	10.15 A.M.	Battalion marched from SWAN CHATEAU to DICKEBUSCH STATION where entrained at 1 P.M. and detrained EBBLINGHEM whence proceeded by march	
CAMPAGNE	—	5.45 P.M.	route to CAMPAGNE arriving 6.45 P.M. in billets.	
— do —	8/1/18		Battalion in billets. Cleaning up and refitting. Reccas to tools etc	
— do —	9/1/18		— do —	
			Company inspections by Commanding Officer. Football match versus 97th Field Ambulance	

Army Form C. 2118.

WAR DIARY
or
INTELLIGENCE SUMMARY.
(Erase heading not required.)

Instructions regarding War Diaries and Intelligence Summaries are contained in F.S. Regs., Part II. and the Staff Manual respectively. Title pages will be prepared in manuscript.

17th (SERVICE) BATT. ORDERLY ROOM 3 FEB. 1918 THE LIVERPOOL REGT.

Place	Date	Hour	Summary of Events and Information	Remarks and references to Appendices
CAMPAGNE	10/1/18		Battalion on little Company Training.	
			His Majesty the King has been graciously pleased to approve of the undermentioned rewards for distinguished and valuable services in the field:-	
			CAPT. C.W. MARSHALL } Military Cross	
			REV.D E.J. WELSHER }	
			16716 L/Sgt. PROCTOR E. Awarded Distinguished Conduct Medal	
			15290 Cpl. RUSSELL B.H. Awarded Meritorious Service Medal	
			(Extract from I.R.O. 3367 26-1-18.)	
			The following are mentioned in the C. in C's Dispatches of 7-11-17 -	
			(6th Sup.t to London Gazette of 14.12.17 N°. 30434.)	
			Temp. Major. C.N. WATSON D.S.O.	
			Captain A.F. TORREY	
			15234 Sgt. W.E. WALTON	
			15421 Cpl. (A/L/Sgt) E.A. WRAY	
CAMPAGNE	11/1/18	P.M. 8.30	Battalion marched from billets in CAMPAGNE to STEENBECQUE Station where entrained at 9.30 p.m. and detrained at LONGUEAU 11.10 p.m. From this	

Army Form C. 2118.

WAR DIARY
or
INTELLIGENCE SUMMARY.
(Erase heading not required.)

Instructions regarding War Diaries and Intelligence Summaries are contained in F. S. Regs., Part II. and the Staff Manual respectively. Title pages will be prepared in manuscript.

17TH (SERVICE) BATT.
ORDERLY ROOM
3 FEB 1918
THE LIVERPOOL REGT.

Place	Date	Hour	Summary of Events and Information	Remarks and references to Appendices
FOUENCAMPS	12/4/18	1.45 a.m.	Joint Battalion marched to billets in FOUENCAMPS arriving 1.45 A.M.	
	13/4/18	10.0 a.m.	Battalion resting and cleaning up for inspection by Corps Commdr.	
do.			Battalion marched from billets in FOUENCAMPS arriving in billets in	
MARCELCAVE	14/4/18	2.30 p.m.	MARCELCAVE at 2.30 p.m.	
do.		2.0 p.m.	Battalion marched from billets in MARCELCAVE at 2 p.m. arriving in billets in	
HARBONNIERES		3.45 p.m.	HARBONNIERES 3.45 P.M.	
do.	15/4/18		Battalion in billets. Platoon drill, Bayonet Fighting, Physical Training	
			A football match was played in the afternoon v. 19th Bn. K.L.R.	
do.	16/4/18		Battalion in billets. The men were pushed at HARBONNIERES Baths.	
			Usual Training carried out by Companies when not bathing	
do.	17/4/18		Battalion in billets. Musketry and extended order drill. Football matches	
			were played in the afternoon v. 2nd Bn. Bedf. Regt. and v 89th M.G.C.	
do.	18/4/18	9.0 a.m.	Battalion marched from billets in HARBONNIERES to DAVENSCOURT arriving	
DAVENSCOURT		2.0 p.m.	2 p.m. in billets	
do.	19/4/18	9.0 a.m.	Battalion marched from billets in DAVENSCOURT to CHAMPIEN arriving	
CHAMPIEN		4.0 p.m.	4 p.m. in billets. Reinforcement 29 O.R.	

Army Form C. 2118.

WAR DIARY
or
INTELLIGENCE SUMMARY.
(Erase heading not required.)

Instructions regarding War Diaries and Intelligence Summaries are contained in F. S. Regs., Part II. and the Staff Manual respectively. Title pages will be prepared in manuscript.

Place	Date	Hour	Summary of Events and Information	Remarks and references to Appendices
CHAMPIEN	20/1/18		Battalion in billets. Cleaning up for inspection by Coy Commanders.	
do	21/1/18		– do – Company Training as arranged by Coy Comdr.	
do	22/1/18		– do – – do –	
do	23/1/18		– do – – do –	
do	24/1/18		Afternoon Football match v. French Aerodrome Staff.	
do	25/1/18		Battalion in billets. Company Training under programme drawn up by Coy. Comdr.	
do			– do – – do –	
do			Divisional Commander inspected training as carried out by "D" Company. Baths at CHAMPIEN allotted for use of Battalion.	
do	26/1/18	10.0 a.m.	Battalion marched from CHAMPIEN at 10 A.M. to billets in LIBERMONT	
		12.30 p.m.	arriving 12.30 p.m.	
LIBERMONT	27/1/18	10.30 p.m.	Battalion marched from LIBERMONT at 10.30 A.M. to billets in MAREST	
do		6.0 p.m.	arriving 6 p.m.	
MAREST	28/1/18	5.0 p.m.	Battalion marched from MAREST at 5 p.m. to billets in VIRY-NOUREUIL	
do		7.0 p.m.	arriving 7 p.m.	
VIRY-NOUREUIL	29/1/18	6.0 p.m.	Battalion marched to relieve the 6th Battn. 338th (French) Infty. Regiment	

WAR DIARY
or
INTELLIGENCE SUMMARY.

(Erase heading not required.)

Army Form C. 2118.

Place	Date	Hour	Summary of Events and Information	Remarks and references to Appendices
VIRY NOUREUIL	29/1/18		In the Line – "B" Company G TRAVECY. "A" Company ST FIRMIN (right.) "B" Company ST FIRMIN (left.) "C" Company in support near Bn HQ	
FRONT LINE	30/1/18	11.15 PM	Relief completed	
– do –	30/1/18		Battalion holding Front Line – ST. FIRMIN – TRAVECY Sector.	
– do –	31/1/18		ditto – – do	

H.E.A Pushman Lt Col.
LIEUT. COLONEL
COMDG. 17th (SERVICE) BATT: THE LIVERPOOL REGT

Vol 28

28.C
6 sheets

CONFIDENTIAL.

WAR DIARY

OF

17th BN. "THE KING'S" (LIVERPOOL REGT).

From 1st FEBRUARY 1918.   To 28th FEBRUARY 1918.

(VOLUME 28.)

Army Form C. 2118.

WAR DIARY
or
INTELLIGENCE SUMMARY.
(Erase heading not required.)

Instructions regarding War Diaries and Intelligence Summaries are contained in F. S. Regs., Part II. and the Staff Manual respectively. Title pages will be prepared in manuscript.

Place	Date	Hour	Summary of Events and Information	Remarks and references to Appendices
ST. FIRMIN – TRAVECY Sector	1/2/18		Battalion holding Front Line	
– do –	2/2/18		– do –	
– do –	3/2/18		– do – Battalion relieved by 19th	
FARGNIER	– " –	9 PM	Battalion K.L.R. Moved to FARGNIER – in Support.	
– do –	4/2/18		Battalion in Support. Providing Working Parties	
– do –	5/2/18		– do –	
– do –	6/2/18		– do –	REINFORCEMENT 12 Officers and 250 other Ranks from 20th K.L.R.
– do –	7/2/18		– do –	
– do –	8/2/18	10.15 pm	Battalion relieved by 2/2nd London Regiment, 58th Division and marched to Billets at CAILLOUEL, arriving 3.15 AM 9/2/18	
CAILLOUEL	9/2/18	8.10 am	Battalion marched from CAILLOUEL to MUIRANCOURT arriving	
MUIRANCOURT	– " –	3.30 pm	in Billets at 3.30 PM.	
– do –	10/2/18	10 am	Battalion marched to AVRICOURT	
AVRICOURT	– " –	1 PM.	Arrived in Billets AVRICOURT	
– do –	11/2/18	9 AM	Morning spent in cleaning and refitting of Equipment &c	
– do –	– " –	2 PM	Battalion paraded for Commanding Officer's inspection	

Army Form C. 2118.

WAR DIARY
or
INTELLIGENCE SUMMARY.
(Erase heading not required.)

Instructions regarding War Diaries and Intelligence Summaries are contained in F. S. Regs., Part II. and the Staff Manual respectively. Title pages will be prepared in manuscript.

Place	Date	Hour	Summary of Events and Information	Remarks and references to Appendices
AVRICOURT	13/2/18	9 am	Companies carried out Physical Drill, Musketry, Bombing and Bayonet Fighting during morning.	
— do —	— " —	2 PM.	Battalion parade for Ceremonial Drill under the Commanding Officer.	
— do —	13/2/18	am.	Battalion marched to ERCHEU district for inspection by Field Marshall Sir DOUGLAS HAIG – Commander-in-Chief.	
— " —	— " —	2.45pm	Inspection by C-in-C took place.	
— " —	— " —	3.30pm	Battalion marched to Billets after inspection.	
— do —	14/2/18	9 am	Companies carried out usual training programme during morning.	
— do —	— " —	2 pm.	All Platoon Commanders paraded for Bayonet Fighting and Physical Training under Sgt. STEEL.	
— do —	— " —	— " —	"A" Company paraded for Ceremonial Drill under Regt. Sgt. Major.	
— do —	— " —	9 PM – 4 PM.	Signalling Class received instruction under Battn. Signalling Officer.	
— do —	15/2/18	9 am.	All Companies carried out Physical Drill, Musketry, Arm and Squad Drill, Bayonet Fighting &c. during the day.	
— do —	— " —			

Army Form C. 2118.

WAR DIARY
or
INTELLIGENCE SUMMARY.

(Erase heading not required.)

Instructions regarding War Diaries and Intelligence Summaries are contained in F. S. Regs., Part II. and the Staff Manual respectively. Title pages will be prepared in manuscript.

Place	Date	Hour	Summary of Events and Information	Remarks and references to Appendices
AVRICOURT.	16/2/18	8 am	Three Companies carried out usual programme of training. One Company fired on Miniature Range during morning. Afternoon - Football Matches.	
- do -	17/2/18		Battalion paraded for Church Services.	
- do -	18/2/18		"B" and "D" Companies trained during the day. Two Companies carried out usual training during day "C" and "D" Companies bathed.	
- do -	19/2/18		Battalion paraded by Companies for bar Demonstration and lecture given by Divisional bar Officer. Three Companies carried out usual training. "C" Company paraded under the R.S.M. for Ceremonial Drill.	
- do -	20/2/18	8.30 am	Battalion marched to FLAVY-LE-MELDEUX (1 Coy at ROUVREL).	
FLAVY-LE-MELDEUX	-	12.30 pm	Arrived in Billets.	
- do -	24/2/18	9.3 am	Battalion marched to AUBIGNY.	
AUBIGNY.	-	1 pm.	Arrived in Billets.	

Army Form C. 2118.

WAR DIARY
or
INTELLIGENCE SUMMARY.
(Erase heading not required.)

Instructions regarding War Diaries and Intelligence Summaries are contained in F. S. Regs., Part II, and the Staff Manual respectively. Title pages will be prepared in manuscript.

Place	Date	Hour	Summary of Events and Information	Remarks and references to Appendices
AUBIGNY.	22/2/18	5. P.M.	Battalion marched to FLUQUIERES.	
FLUQUIERES	"	6 P.M.	Arrived in Billets	
- do -	23/2/18		Battalion in Support. Providing Working Parties for work in BATTLE ZONE. Digging Trenches, wiring &c.	
- do -	24/2/18		ditto	
- do -	25/2/18		ditto	
- do -	26/2/18		ditto	
- do -	27/2/18		ditto	
- do -		9 P.M.	Practice "Stand to" carried out. (Battalion arrangement)	
- do -	28/2/18	5.45am	Test message "Man Battle Position" received from Brigade. Battalion moved up to BATTLE ZONE to 'Stand to'.	
- do -		7.15am	All Companies in position. Returned to Billets.	
- do -		11.15am	Order "Take preparatory action" received from Brigade. Battalion stood to in readiness to move off at a moments notice.	

AMarshall Capt
for LIEUT. COLONEL
COMDG 17TH (SERVICE) BATTN THE LIVERPOOL REGT

89th Inf.Bde.
30th Div.

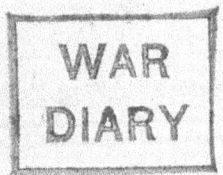

17th BATTN. THE KING'S (LIVERPOOL REGIMENT).

M A R C H

1 9 1 8

CONFIDENTIAL.

WAR DIARY.

OF

17TH BATTALION "THE KING'S" (LIVERPOOL REGIMENT.)

FROM MARCH 1ST 1918 TO MARCH 31ST 1918.

VOLUME No. 29.

Army Form C. 2118.

WAR DIARY
or
INTELLIGENCE SUMMARY.
(Erase heading not required.)

Instructions regarding War Diaries and Intelligence Summaries are contained in F. S. Regs., Part II. and the Staff Manual respectively. Title pages will be prepared in manuscript.

Place	Date	Hour	Summary of Events and Information	Remarks and references to Appendices
ST. QUENTIN Right Sub-Sector	1/3/18	P.M. 9.10	The Battalion relieved the 18TH Battalion (L.H.) H.L.R. with "B" Company on RIGHT. "D" Company on RIGHT — "C" Company on LEFT. "B" Company — COUNTER ATTACK — "A" Company PASSIVE RESISTANCE. Battalion H.Q. in quarry behind L'ÉPINE DE DALLON redoubt.	
— " —	2/3/18	A.M. 12.10	Battalion H.Q. transferred forward to the redoubt. Combined patrols sent out to become acquainted with features of NO MAN'S LAND and to obtain an identification. No enemy encountered.	
— " —	3/3/18	P.M. 4.0	Battalion H.Q. removed back to the Quarry. Battalion holding the line. Major Jompfer and General Staff reconnoitred gaps on the wire in front of the line of redoubts (GAY TRENCH, GRANVILLE TRENCH and TRENCH HAVRE) with view to having moveable obstacles made to fill in. Usual patrols sent out and work on trenches and wire	
— " —	4/3/18		Battalion holding the line. Work on wire dug-out and making of wire obstacles.	
— " —	5/3/18	A.M. 4.45	At about 4.45 A.M. enemy barrage was put along our Right Company front in form of box barrage covering forward line, C.T.S. and	

WAR DIARY
or
INTELLIGENCE SUMMARY.

(Erase heading not required.)

Army Form C. 2118.

Place	Date	Hour	Summary of Events and Information	Remarks and references to Appendices
ST. QUENTIN R. Sub-sector	5/3/18		and rear line also neighbourhood of Company HQ. Trench mortars were fired into wire near CANAL about A.6.a.4.8. and 4.7.5. and 5.9.'s were employed on trenches. Barrage lasted until 5.30 A.M. At about 4.50 A.M. enemy entered our forward trench about A.6.a. 4.9 through gap in wire above mentioned. This shot is in between two of our posts. Previous to entering trench enemy was not heard or seen by these posts. Enemy proceeded along behind our No 1 post on CANAL at A.6.a.40.75 and a hand to hand fight took place / bombs and rifles being employed, during which all men on this post were wounded except two who are reported missing. One wounded Boche was left in our trench. Enemy was only in our trenches apparently for about 10 minutes and did not proceed elsewhere. The post on the immediate left hearing scuffle proceeded to close in in that direction. The foremost man was seen to be hit and the post was driven back by bombing. This man is also missing. The S.O.S. was sent up from all front posts and was answered in about 5 minutes.	

Army Form C. 2118.

WAR DIARY
or
INTELLIGENCE SUMMARY.
(Erase heading not required.)

Place	Date	Hour	Summary of Events and Information	Remarks and references to Appendices
ST. QUENTIN R. Sub-sector	5/3/18		A post at S.29.d.6.9 reports seeing enemy coming over "in mass" along our wire and fired on them. The Lewis Gun at S.29.d.8.6 fired across front. Prisoner captured belonged to 210th Infantry Bn. (100th Storming Coy.) which was brought up specially for this raid. He had been in this sector for 10 days and knew very little about artillery. Raiding party consisted of about 150 men. Casualties Missing 2 O.R. Wounded 7 O.R.	
"	6/3/18		Battalion holding the line. Making obstacles and filling in gaps in wire.	
"	7/3/18		Our artillery bombarded enemy trench systems and M.G. emplacements. Battalion holding the line. Usual patrols and work on gaps and trenches carried out. Harassing fire on enemy roads and trenches by artillery.	
"	8/3/18		Battalion holding the line. Patrolling, wiring etc carried out.	
"	9/3/18	10.0 p.m.	Battalion relieved in St. QUENTIN sector by 19th Bn. K.L.R. Relief complete and Battalion marched to support positions at VAUX, being responsible for the defence of 4 D. South sub-sector of the BATTLE ZONE.	
VAUX	10/3/18		Battalion in support. Cleaning up and training. Inspection of rifles	

WAR DIARY
or
INTELLIGENCE SUMMARY.
(Erase heading not required.)

Army Form C. 2118.

Place	Date	Hour	Summary of Events and Information	Remarks and references to Appendices
VAUX	10/3/18	(cont'd)	by the Divisional Armourer Sergeant. All Officers and N.C.O's reconnoitred the Battle Zone.	
"	11/3/18		Battalion in support. Every available man paraded for work on the Battle Zone under R.E. supervision.	
"	12/3/18	P.M. 3.30	Battalion in support. Intensive training carried out. All Officers and N.C.O's attend a lecture at FLUQUIERES by Brig. Genl. the Hon. F.C. STANLEY. D.S.O.	
"	13/3/18		Battalion in support. Every available man paraded for work on the Battle Zone. A football match was played versus 98th Field Ambulance.	
"	14/3/18		Battalion in support. Intensive training carried out.	
"	15/3/18		do Every available man paraded for work on the Battle Zone.	
"	16/3/18		Battalion in support. Every available man paraded for work on the Battle Zone. Vaccination of the Battalion carried out.	
"	17/3/18		Battalion in support. Divine service. Officers & N.C.O's carried out a tactical scheme on the Battle Zone. During period in support daily reconnaissance of the Battle Zone was made.	

Army Form C. 2118.

WAR DIARY
or
INTELLIGENCE SUMMARY.
(Erase heading not required.)

Place	Date	Hour	Summary of Events and Information	Remarks and references to Appendices
VAUX	18/9/18	6.0 P.M.	Battalion relieved in support position by 17th Bn Manchester Regiment and	
VILLERS ST. CHRISTOPHE	" "	8.5	marched to billets in VILLERS ST. CHRISTOPHE arriving 8.5 P.M.	
"	19/9/18		Battalion in Billets. Cleaning and training.	
"	20/9/18		— do —	
"	21/9/18	5.16 A.M.	Orders received to leave VILLERS ST CHRISTOPHE for BEAVOIS, dig in defence	
BEAVOIS			round village and organised same for defence. Enemy shelled village intermittently throughout the day but little damage was done.	
ATILLY		10.30 P.M.	Marched to ATILLY and came under General WHITE, 184th Infy Bde. (61 D.) Two Companies and Bn. H.G. in railway cutting N.W. of ATILLY – Two Companies in Counter Attack positions at SWORD WOOD.	
"	22/9/18	6.30 A.M.	Sent "D" Company (CAPT. E.P.BEAUMONT M.C.) to 2/5th Glor. Reg't in HOLNON WOOD to counter attack part of Battle Zone. Company to be under orders of O.C. 2/5th Glouc'rs. This Company drove enemy from the trenches they occupied and consolidated the position. Morning very misty.	
"		10.30 A.M.	Orders received to move Battalion to AVIATION WOOD – Carried out under	

Army Form C. 2118.

WAR DIARY
or
INTELLIGENCE SUMMARY.
(Erase heading not required.)

Instructions regarding War Diaries and Intelligence Summaries are contained in F. S. Regs., Part II. and the Staff Manual respectively. Title pages will be prepared in manuscript.

Place	Date	Hour	Summary of Events and Information	Remarks and references to Appendices
AVIATION WOOD	22/3/18	2.30 p.m.	Heavy hostile shell fire. On arrival at AVIATION WOOD it was found that H.Q. 21st Infy. Bde. had left. "B" and H.Q. Companies in position on sunken road E of wood and on enemy commencing strong attack on FLUQUIERES remainder of Battalion deployed W of wood. At about 6.30 p.m. orders received that all troops of 30th Division	
HAM	" "	9.30 p.m.	should withdraw to HAM. Reached HAM about 9.30 p.m. Orders received that Battalion should take up half of the defence of HAM. Major Emery joined the Battn. he having previously reconnoitred the position. Battn. H.Q. established in position near north bridge where R.E. Officer detailed to blow up the bridges joined the Battalion. Battalion	
"	23/3/18		in defensive positions N of HAM. Troops of 20th Division passed through the town during the hours MIDNIGHT to 3 a.m. having received orders to withdraw.	
"	" "	6.30 a.m.	Our troops began to retire through the town and gave information that the enemy had broken through on their flanks and at 7 a.m. the bridge north of HAM was blown up. Slow retirement made through	

Army Form C. 2118.

WAR DIARY
or
INTELLIGENCE SUMMARY.
(Erase heading not required.)

Instructions regarding War Diaries and Intelligence Summaries are contained in F. S. Regs., Part II. and the Staff Manual respectively. Title pages will be prepared in manuscript.

Place	Date	Hour	Summary of Events and Information	Remarks and references to Appendices
HAM.	22/3/18		the town the enemy having apparently entered from the South Eastern end and being well inside the town.	
—	—	7.30 A.M.	The South bridge blown up. Morning very misty and difficult to distinguish our troops from enemy.	
			In conjunction with 18th Bn K.L.R. position established N.E. of	
VERLAINES	—	8.30 A.M.	VERLAINES. During the morning our troops advanced and established a position on crest of hill S.W. of HAM in spite of heavy machine gun fire. Two enemy M.G.'s captured and enemy aeroplane which had been flying low over our positions was brought down by rifle fire. Hostile machine guns and enemy aeroplanes very active, also enemy artillery especially W. and S. of VERLAINES. Battn H.Q. in sunken road abt 200 yds N.E. of VERLAINES.	
—	—	About 12 noon	details of 61st Division passed through position occupied by Bn H.Q. under orders to capture VERLAINES. They went forward to positions occupied by our troops and dug in on the left of our position. Their positions were reconnoitred and found to be very	

WAR DIARY
or
INTELLIGENCE SUMMARY.

(Erase heading not required.)

Army Form C. 2118.

Place	Date	Hour	Summary of Events and Information	Remarks and references to Appendices
VERLAINES	24/3/18		unsatisfactory, and it was arranged that he should turn out and deploy his troops more to the left, only being extended to keep joined up with him.	
"	"		In the early hours of the morning enemy made a strong attack on our forward posts on W of HAM – ESMERY HALLON road but were driven off and a prisoner captured. Shortly after enemy enfiladed R.R. position with Machine Gun and rifle fire. Enemy was then observed coming through on the left flank, and orders were issued to Corps to withdraw, fighting a rear guard action on ESMERY – HALLON. Stand was made on sunken road S of VERLAINES where enemy was kept in check for half an hour, after which a rear guard action was fought and positions eventually taken up along with other troops in front of canal W of ESMERY – HALLON. Later in the night defensive positions were dug and taken up East of MOYENCOURT., along with 18TH and 19TH Bns. K.L.R., Trench Mortar unit and details of 21st Infy. Bde.	
ESMERY HALLON	24/3/18			
MOYENCOURT	" "			

WAR DIARY or INTELLIGENCE SUMMARY.

Army Form C. 2118.

(Erase heading not required.)

Place	Date	Hour	Summary of Events and Information	Remarks and references to Appendices
MOYENCOURT	25/3/18		Enemy Artillery active during the day — 4 Officers and 80 O.R. were attached to Col Whitehead (16th Manchester) about 4.30 P.M. orders received to withdraw which were carried out under considerable enemy shelling. One Company being left to cover retreat "remainder" of the Battalion (except detached with 16th Manchester) marched to ROIGLISE where they embussed to PLESSIER and then relied for the night.	
ROIGLISE				
PLESSIER	26/3/18		The Company attached to 16th Manchesters remained in the front line until 6.50 P.M. and then withdrew to CRESSY. During the morning the Battalion moved to FOLIES and took up positions west of the village. Later on 2 Companies under Capt. RIGBY-JONES were ordered to man the Donne trenches E. of ROUVROY the remaining Company occupying trenches N.E. of FOLIES.	
PLESSIER	-"-			
FOLIES	-"-			
-"-	-"-		Battn. H.Q. in dug outs just west of the village	
-"-	27/3/18		Orders received that Battalion with the exception of 2 Companies at ROUVROY were to march to HANGEST and take up defensive positions there. N.B. Company went forward. The remaining Company	

Army Form C. 2118.

WAR DIARY
or
INTELLIGENCE SUMMARY.
(Erase heading not required.)

Place	Date	Hour	Summary of Events and Information	Remarks and references to Appendices
FOLIES	27/3/18		On arriving at strong point near wood in K 15 was ordered by Genl Stevens (90th Brigade) to man that strong point. In the afternoon orders were received to occupy position E. of BOUCHOIR — WARVILLERS road with this Company in conjunction with 18th Bn K.R.R. and 2nd Bn Yorks. Regt. — Part of H.Q. Company returned about 5.30 p.m. the remainder having been ordered to take up defensive position in HANGEST. Hostile shelling continued during	
—	28/3/18 A.M.		the night, increasing in volume during the following morning.	
		10.0	Enemy attacked our immediate front but was driven off — Half an hour later enemy was seen in large numbers advancing through	
		11.0 A.M.	ROUVROY to WARVILLERS. — About 11 a.m. orders were received that the Battalion would be relieved by the 133rd French Division — The relief was carried out shortly after noon, after a message had been received by telephone that the French were entrusted with the position and that we were to withdraw at once — The enemy	
MEZIERES	—	4.0 p.m.	were then in BEAUFORT — The Battalion assembled at MEZIERES	

Army Form C. 2118.

WAR DIARY
or
INTELLIGENCE SUMMARY.
(Erase heading not required.)

Instructions regarding War Diaries and Intelligence Summaries are contained in F. S. Regs., Part II. and the Staff Manual respectively. Title pages will be prepared in manuscript.

Place	Date	Hour	Summary of Events and Information	Remarks and references to Appendices
ROUVREL	29/8/18	P.M. 6.30	and marched to ROUVREL. (i) fillets arriving about 6.30 P.M.	
"	29/8/18		Battalion in billets. Composite Battalion formed consisting of elements from 17th 18th and 19th Bns. K.L.R. and Trench Mortar unit.	
"	30/8/18	A.M. 9.15	Battalion moved by march route to SOLEUX where they entrained for ST VALERY SUR SOMME and billed there for the night.	
ST VALERY SUR SOMME	31/8/18		The Composite Battalion was disbanded and the elements thereof rejoined their respective Battalions. The Battalion then marched	
NIBAS	"	P.M. 1.15	to billets in NIBAS arriving at 1.15 P.M.	

J. Richards ? LIEUT. COLONEL
COMMDG 17TH (SERVICE) BATT. THE LIVERPOOL REGT

Vol 30 89/30

90 C
9 sheets

CONFIDENTIAL.

WAR DIARY.

of

17TH BATTALION "THE KINGS" (LIVERPOOL REGIMENT.)

From 1st APRIL 1918. to 30th APRIL 1918.

VOLUME XXX.

Army Form C. 2118.

WAR DIARY
or
INTELLIGENCE SUMMARY.

(Erase heading not required.)

Instructions regarding War Diaries and Intelligence Summaries are contained in F. S. Regs., Part II. and the Staff Manual respectively. Title pages will be prepared in manuscript.

Place	Date	Hour	Summary of Events and Information	Remarks and references to Appendices
NIBAS	APRIL 1st	-	Companies paraded during the day for Training, Reorganisation, and cleaning up.	
ST.VALERY-SUR- SOMME REF MAP:-				
ABBEVILLE SHEET - 14 1:100.000	2nd	-	Parades as on the 1st instant.	
	3rd	-	Companies paraded for training under Company Commanders.	
	4th	10. PM	The 17th K.L.R. marched from NIBAS to VOINCOURT and proceeded by train to PROVEN from there moving by 'Bus to BRIDGE CAMP No 1	
		12. PM		
BRIDGE CAMP No.1 ELVERDINGHE B.19.d. SHEET 28.1:40.000	5th	8.15AM	ELVERDINGE Training for the day was carried out under Company Commanders. Lewis Gunners being instructed separately under Sgt. Bryan.	
	6th	-		
	7th	-	In accordance with Bdn Operation Orders, Battn Operation Order 128 was issued and the 17th K.L.R. entrained at ELVERDINGHE YARD and proceeded to VARNA.FM.(C.4.a.5.2) the detraining point, marching from there to the POELCAPPELLE SECTOR SUPPORT LINE in relief of the 1st Battn Cameron Highlanders. 1st Battn Loyal North Lancs. Regt. both of the 1st Div. Brigade – Batts throughout being situated at PIG and WHISTLE Batts in support line – Details accomodated at BECKWITH CAMP (B.7.b.)	
POELCAPPELLE - SECTOR - SUPPORT LINE	8th			

Army Form C. 2118.

WAR DIARY
or
INTELLIGENCE SUMMARY.
(Erase heading not required.)

Instructions regarding War Diaries and Intelligence Summaries are contained in F. S. Regs., Part II, and the Staff Manual respectively. Title pages will be prepared in manuscript.

Place	Date	Hour	Summary of Events and Information	Remarks and references to Appendices
	APRIL			
POELCAPPELLE – SECTOR – SUPPORT LINE	9th		Batln in Support Line.	
	10th		Batln in Support Line.	
POELCAPPELLE SECTOR: FRONT LINE SYSTEM.	11th		In accordance with Batln O.O. 129 the 17th K.R.R. were relieved in the "Support line" by the 19th K.R.R. - Upon relief the 17th K.R.R. moved to the "Front line System" in relief of the 18th K.R.R. - Batln Headquarters being accommodated at SOUVENIR HOUSE	
— " —	12th		Operation Order 130 was issued and the 17th K.R.R. took over the Support Zone meanwhile holding allotted posts in the Forward Zone. Batln Headquarters moved to VARNA FARM.	
POELCAPPELLE SECTOR FORWARD SUPPORT ZONES	13th		Patrolling was vigorous during the night	
— " —	14th		A quantity of Bombs, S.A.A. & R.E. materials was salved during the day & taken to the Divisional Dump.	
— " —	15th		Batalion in Forward Support Zone – Salvage of R.E. material was continued	
— " —	16th		In accordance with Hyper Plans – Batln Operation Order 131 was issued & the 17th K.R.R. withdrew to the line of the STEENBEEK at 3. a.m. on	

Sticky note:
See my notes
I am much inclined
to think that 17th Apl. should
read 16th — 18th Ap. should
read 17th, 7.30 a.m.
Des?

WAR DIARY
or
INTELLIGENCE SUMMARY.
(Erase heading not required.)

Instructions regarding War Diaries and Intelligence Summaries are contained in F.S. Regs., Part II. and the Staff Manual respectively. Title pages will be prepared in manuscript.

Place	Date	Hour	Summary of Events and Information
LENNOX CAMP (B.7.c.5.5.) SHEET 28.N.E. 1:20,000	APRIL 17th	7 am	The morning of the 17th — on completion of withdrawal, Companies marched independently to LENNOX CAMP arriving about 7 am.
		7.30 pm	Balln. embussed at LENNOX CAMP & proceeded to WESTOUTRE —
WESTOUTRE — MONT. KOKEREEL ROAD (M.8.d.) SHEET 28.S.E. 1:20,000	18th		MONT. KOKEREEL Road where debussing took place at 10.30 pm. The Battalion Bivouacced at the roadside overnight. Baln. remained at the Roadside as Corps Reserve.
		8 pm	The 17th K.R.R. proceeded at 8 pm to the Front Line south east of ST. JANS. CAPPEL in relief of a unit of the 101st Manch. Brigade. Baln. inadequate Army accommodation in chateau (M.32.c.0/9).
FRONT LINE SOUTH EAST ST. JANS CAPPEL SHEET 28.S.W. 1:20,000	19th		Patrolling was vigorous — 2/Lieut Regill, M.C. M.M., proceeded on patrol with 5 other Ranks — and enemy party was met shots were exchanged & 2/Lieut Gill was hit in the head and fell into a ditch, the remainder of the party returned 4.15 am to our lines, a further party of 8 other Ranks led by 2nd Lieut Cook was sent upon from a distance of 10 yards 2nd Lieut Cook was badly wounded also one other rank — efforts to save him proved futile owing to intensity of enemy fire.

Army Form C. 2118.

WAR DIARY
or
INTELLIGENCE SUMMARY.
(Erase heading not required.)

Place	Date	Hour	Summary of Events and Information	Remarks and references to Appendices
R.11.b SHEET 28 27 SE 1. 20.000	APRIL 20th	—	In accordance with Battn Operation Order 132 the 17th K.R.R. was relieved in the Front Line by the 23rd Company of the 321st Inf. Regt. (French Army) upon completion of relief the Battalion marched to Anzal wood. about R.11.b and proceeded to the remainder of the night. The Bombing Officer (Lieut Col Crookston DSO) was wounded & taken to hospital (20.4.18)	
BUSSEBOOM SCOTTISH CAMP DOMINION CAMP (G.22.b) SHEET 28 NW 23rd 1. 20.000	21st	8.30 am	The 17th K.R.R. marched to SCOTTISH and DOMINION CAMPS, BUSSEBOOM. Battn headquarters being in SCOTTISH CAMP Companies were inspected by the Officer Commanding 17th K.R.R. commencing at 11 a.m.	
	22nd		The 17th K.R.R. provided working parties employing 11 Officers + 350 Other Ranks to work with the 200th Field Coy. Royal Engineers. A General Clean of unfit arms was carried out under Sgt Bryan for inspection. The following particulars of awards granted to Officers, NCOs + Men of the 17th K.R.R. are extracted from Battn Routine Orders 2/22/4/18	

Army Form C. 2118.

WAR DIARY
or
INTELLIGENCE SUMMARY.
(Erase heading not required.)

Place	Date	Hour	Summary of Events and Information	Remarks and references to Appendices
SCOTTISH & DOMINION CAMPS. BUSSEBOOM	APRIL 23rd		Officers:- awards:- Lieut. Col. Enderton D.S.O. - Bar to D.S.O. Capt. – E. Rigby-Jones – Military Cross. Capt. – E.A. Dickson – Military Cross. N.C.O's and men:- 49137 Sgt. Stobbing. W. – Distinguished Conduct Medal. 15755 Sgt. Bryan E.G. – Military Medal. 48396 L/Cpl. Baldwin J. – ditto – 51996 Pte. Innes H.M. – ditto – 51897 Pte. Argile R. – ditto – 57936 Pte. Lewis S. – ditto –	
– do –	APRIL 24th		Working parties were provided in accordance with Schedule issued in Battn. Routine Order 130 d/23-4-18.	
– do –	APRIL 25th		The Battalion warned at 2.30 A.M. to move at half an hour's notice to position of readiness. This was done at about 3 P.M. and	

WAR DIARY or INTELLIGENCE SUMMARY

Army Form C. 2118.

Place	Date	Hour	Summary of Events and Information	Remarks and references to Appendices
VOORMEZEELE SECTOR	APRIL 25TH		Positions taken up N of DICKEBUSCH. The Bn. Details moved at the same time to ST LAWRENCE CAMP. Battalion returned to SCOTTISH and DOMINION CAMPS same night.	
"	26TH		The Battalion again moved to positions of readiness at 4 A.M. and returned to SCOTTISH and DOMINION CAMPS same night.	
"	27TH	8.30 P.M.	The Battalion moved to the line in relief of No 4 Battalion (39TH Composite Brigade) and relief completed about 1 A.M. (28TH inst.)	
"	28TH		At about 1 P.M. a Company at Composite Bn. gave way on the left of our line and the Boches penetrated from the Canal Bank to left of my Battalion front, which position he maintained despite 5 hours fighting. My reserve Company was ordered to counter-attack and restore the position at 7.45 P.M., his enemy laid down a barrage at 7.43 A.M. and the counter attack was unable to proceed. The enemy bombardment lasted until 10.30 P.M., and I then organised a defensive flank.	
"	29TH		At 3.30 A.M. heavy enemy bombardment opened, followed later by	

WAR DIARY
or
INTELLIGENCE SUMMARY.

Army Form C. 2118.

(Erase heading not required.)

Place	Date	Hour	Summary of Events and Information	Remarks and references to Appendices
VOORMEZEELE DEFENCES	APRIL 29	9.0 a.m.	enemy attack and our line was forced back to G.H.Q. 1 where I reorganised and held on to the position. The enemy got enough on both flanks practically surrounding 2 of my Companies. "A" Company was actively surrounded and after severe fighting were captured.	
"	30th		The Battalion still holding G.H.Q. 1 line. At various times during the day small parties of the enemy crept forward with Machine Guns and were engaged by Lewis Guns and Rifle fire. Also concentrations of enemy were dispersed by Artillery shoots.	
			Total casualties during operations 29/4/18 – 30/4/18.	
			2/Lieut T. HARROP Killed 28/4/18 17 O.R. Killed in Action.	
			Capt. R.H. BLOORE do 28/4/18 80 O.R. Wounded.	
			Lieut. H. MEYER Wounded 29/4/18 1 O.R. Gassed.	
			2/Lieut A.H. ELLIS Missing 29/4/18 2 O.R. Wounded Missing	
			Lieut. E.S. ASHCROFT Wounded & Missing 15/1/18 } 177 O.R. Missing	

relieved from Bn. H.Q.

Toff Manuiter Capt. for LIEUT COL
COMDG 17TH BN "THE KING'S" (LIVERPOOL REGT.)

No. 31

31.C
7 sheets
1st to 31st May 1918

CONFIDENTIAL

WAR DIARY

OF

17TH BATTALION "THE KING'S" (L'POOL REG'T)

FOR THE MONTH OF MAY - 1918 -

VOLUME XXXI

Army Form C. 2118.

WAR DIARY
or
INTELLIGENCE SUMMARY.
(Erase heading not required.)

Instructions regarding War Diaries and Intelligence Summaries are contained in F. S. Regs., Part II. and the Staff Manual respectively. Title pages will be prepared in manuscript.

Place	Date	Hour	Summary of Events and Information	Remarks and references to Appendices
VOORMEZEELE DEFENCES.	1/5/18.		Battalion relieved by the 1st Bn. Cheshire Regiment and moved to SCOTTISH CAMP, arriving about 2 am on 2nd inst.	Ref. Map.
SCOTTISH CAMP.	2/5/18.	Noon.	Battalion moved to ST. LAWRENCE CAMP, near BRANDHOEK.	BRANDHOEK.
ST. LAWRENCE CAMP.	— " —		The Brigade (17th, 18th and 19th K.L.R.) was formed into a Composite Battalion by Lieut. Col. G. ROLLO. D.S.O. — 17th (Composite) Bn. K.L.R. and was commanded on formation about 27 offrs. 750 o.r. Fighting Strength on formation about 27 offrs. 750 o.r. 17th K.L.R. formed "A" Coy. 18th K.L.R. — "B" Coy. 19th K.L.R. — "C" Coy. "D" Company was made up by elements of the 3 Battalions. Battalion in ST. LAWRENCE CAMP. — Cleaning up and re-organising, etc.	Sheet 28. 1/40,000.
do	3/5/18		— do —	
— " —	4/5/18.		— ditto —	
— " —	5/5/18.	10.45 PM	Battalion commenced to move to Forward Zone in front of VIERSTRAAT, and took up positions in Brigade Reserve on the LA CLYTTE — HALLEBAST CORNER — line. Battalion Headquarters — MICMAC CAMP. Enemy artillery active throughout the day.	
VIERSTRAAT SECTOR Bde. Reserve	6/5/18.		Heavy enemy shelling with H.E. and Gas shells.	
— do —	7/5/18.			
— do —	8/5/18.	9 AM	Advanced Batn. HQ. established by Major J.P. PITTS. and 2/Lieut. J. HODGSON.	
— do —	— " —	2.45 PM	"A" and "B" Coys. were moved forward to a position of readiness on Reserve line from N. 3. V. Central. to N. 3. d. 7/0.	
— do —	— " —	3.15 PM	5th Bn. Scottish Rifles reached Battalion Headquarters at G. 36. b. 3/4.	
— do —	— " —	4.30 PM	Klein Battalion Headquarters through KLEIN VIERSTRAAT CABARET (N.10.a.3/5) to N.4.d. 7.0/9.5. with Front line run HALLE BAST LINE. (LA CLYTTE — HALLE BAST LINE) with	

Army Form C. 2118.

WAR DIARY
or
INTELLIGENCE SUMMARY.
(Erase heading not required.)

Instructions regarding War Diaries and Intelligence Summaries are contained in F. S. Regs., Part II. and the Staff Manual respectively. Title pages will be prepared in manuscript.

Place	Date	Hour	Summary of Events and Information	Remarks and references to Appendices
VIERSTRAAT SECTOR - BDE RESERVE.	8/5/18.	4.30 P.M.	Enemy in our original front line.	Ref. Map. Sheet 28. 1/40,000.
	-"-	6.30 P.M.	19th Infy. Brigade in conjunction with the French (32nd Division) were ordered to deliver attack with object of retaking original line from N.10.c 7/9 - S.W. corner of RIDGE WOOD. One Battalion (5th Scottish Rifles) to attack at 7 P.M. in a Southerly direction from the GENERAL LINE GORDON FARM to RIDGE WOOD. Objective - original front line to HALLEBAST CORNER - VIERSTRAAT ROAD line. One Battalion (Cameronians) with 32nd French Division on Right, to cross the line of the VIVERBEEK with their left on the HALLEBAST - VIERSTRAAT ROAD. Artillery to keep up a steady rate of fire on our original front line until 6.30 P.M. Between 6.30 P.M. & 7 P.M. fire to gradually increase 7 P.M. - 7.15 P.M. Intense bombardment lifting at 7.25 P.M. on to our original S.O.S. line. French Artillery to co-operate in support of their advancing troops. The line dealt by us ran - along VIVERBEEK - KLEIN VIERSTRAAT, with Support line in N.14.d. - South West corner of RIDGE WOOD. Thence along original front line.	
		7.10 P.M.	French Troops started to advance. No troops being observed advancing with their left along the HALLEBAST - VIERSTRAAT ROAD, "A" and "B" Coys. 17th (Comp) Bn. K.L.R. were ordered to move forward in artillery formation from support line in N.3.d. with object of co-operating with the French troops.	
		8.10 P.M.	Counter-attack reported by Adv. Battn. H.Q. to be going well on the left but nothing could be seen on the right.	
		8.45 P.M.	Scottish Rifles and French Troops reported to have passed over the	

Army Form C. 2118.

WAR DIARY
or
INTELLIGENCE SUMMARY.
(Erase heading not required.)

Place	Date	Hour	Summary of Events and Information	Remarks and references to Appendices
VIERSTRAAT SECTOR.	8/5/18	8.45 p.m.	Ridge originally held us in the morning of 8th inst.	
		9.25 p.m.	Prisoners (1 Officer + 6 men) captured by "A" Company.	
		10.30 p.m.	Situation reported to be as follows:— One party composed of 2 Officers, 17th K.L.R. and 30 men of several units held a line from N.10.a.9/6 – N.10.b.1/9. Another composite party above 40 strong held a line from above N.4.d.3/5 – N.4.d.5/9. A 2nd line was being held from above N.3.b.7/5 to N.9.a.9/8. by 2nd YORKS. This line was in touch with 2nd BEDFORDS and NEW ZEALAND RIFLES on the left. 8 machine guns. Right and French on the Right. Reinforcements were badly needed before dawn if forward positions were to be held.	
– do –	9/5/18	2.40 a.m.	Message received from Brigade H.Q. timed 1.0 am stating objectives appeared to have been gained. 2nd BEDFORDS and 2nd YORKS. were ordered to withdraw.	
		4.0 a.m.	Two Companies 17th K.L.R. moved forward in ones and twos to re-establish a line from N.10.c.8/8 to N.10.b.9/6. Line failed to do so before daylight. Bde. Sector was reorganised — Dispositions of Brigade Front line were:— N.10.a.0/0. (liaison has been obtained with the French at this point). from N.10.a.5/4 – N.10.a.7/0 – N.10.a.5/4. held by "D" Coy. 17th K.L.R.; from N.10.b.15/90 to N.10.b.80/85 by 2 Platoons of "C" Coy. 17th K.L.R. from N.10.b.15/90 to N.10.b.80/85 by 2 Platoons of "C" Coy. 17th K.L.R. At this point Battn. are in touch with "A" Coy. 4th K.L.R. (attached to 5th Scottish Rifles) from N.10.b.85/85 to N.5.c.10/65 is held by this Company of 4th K.L.R. and from N.5.c.70/20 (South end of RIDGE WOOD) by 5th Scottish Rifles.	
		5.40 p.m.		

Army Form C. 2118.

WAR DIARY
or
INTELLIGENCE SUMMARY.
(Erase heading not required.)

Instructions regarding War Diaries and Intelligence Summaries are contained in F.S. Regs., Part II. and the Staff Manual respectively. Title pages will be prepared in manuscript.

Place	Date	Hour	Summary of Events and Information	Remarks and references to Appendices
VIERSTRAAT SECTOR.	9/5/18	5.40 P.M.	Enemy reported to be 200 yards in front of N.E. and S.W. in N.10.a. "C" Coy. 17th K.L.R. (less 2 Platoons) holding Reserve Line N.B.g.7/5. along road running Scuick to N.9.a 9/9. This line has liaison on the night with the French and on the left with the New Zealand Rifles. 17th K.L.R. was relieved from Forward Zone by the 1st Queen's and 120th Brigade Reserve Position again on the LA CYTTE - HALLEBAST - CORNER ROAD LINE.	
— do —	10/5/18		Battalion relieved by the 1st QUEEN'S. and moved back to ST. LAWRENCE CAMP.	
ST. LAWRENCE CAMP.	11/5/18	10 A.M.	Battn. arrived in Camp. During period 5/5/18 - 10/5/18. following Casualties were sustained:- 17th K.L.R. Killed; 8/5/1918.]10 o.R. Killed. Capt. N. Henry M.C. Wounded & Missing 8/5/18.]37 o.R. Wounded. 2Lt. A.H. Black. 19 o.R. Missing.	
— do —	—	5 P.M.	Battalion entrained on the POPERINGHE - ABEELE Road, and moved to BUYSSCHEURE - detraining at about 7.30 P.M.	
BUYSSCHEURE	—	7.30 P.M.	In Camp at BUYSSCHEURE. Day spent in cleaning up after	
— do —	12/5/18			
— do —	13/5/18		Battalion Transport moved to CWCQ. (Transport Depot) for disposal by G.H.Q. on account of Unit being reduced to a Training Cadre.	
— do —	14/5/18		4 Officers and 218 Other Ranks despatched to 'G' Base Depot. ETAPLES. as Surplus to Training Establishment.	
— do —	15/5/18	10.20 A.M.	Battalion Training Staff marched to AUDRUICQ, where entrained for WOINCOURT.	
WOINCOURT	16/5/18	9 A.M.	Detrained. Marched to Billets in MENESLIES. arriving about 10 A.M.	

Army Form C. 2118.

WAR DIARY
or
INTELLIGENCE SUMMARY.
(Erase heading not required.)

Instructions regarding War Diaries and Intelligence Summaries are contained in F. S. Regs., Part II. and the Staff Manual respectively. Title pages will be prepared in manuscript.

Place	Date	Hour	Summary of Events and Information	Remarks and references to Appendices
MENESLIES.	17/5/18		Training Staff affiliated to the 1st Bn. 137th Infantry Regt. (U.S. Army) for Training purposes.	
– do –	18/5/18		In Billets. Training arrangements made with the American Unit, and programmes discussed, and drawn up for coming week.	
– do –	19/5/18		– do –	
– do –	20/5/18		Training commenced. Instruction given each day in :— Musketry, Bayonet Training, Lewis Gun Instruction, Gas Drill, Field Fortifications, Tactical Exercises by Platoons. Each day one Company paraded on a Route March to Ault, Machines American Guards and Rearguard. Lectures en route and Rearguard and N.C.O. Instructors each evening	
– do –	21/5/18			
– do –	22/5/18			
– do –	23/5/18			
– do –	24/5/18			
– do –	25/5/18			
– do –	26/5/18	2 P.M.	Lectures were given by various Officers on various Subjects. Training Staff marched to INCHEVILLE for affiliation to 3rd Bn. 138th Infantry Regiment (U.S. Army).	
INCHEVILLE.	– " –	4.30 P.M.	Arrived in Billets. Programme of Training drawn up and discussed with American Battn Commander.	
– do –	27/5/18		Training carried out on lines laid down for 1st Bn. 137th Infantry Regt. – 1st week's Training.	
– do –	28/5/18			
– do –	29/5/18		This day recognised as a holiday for U.S.A. Troops. Issue Training carried out.	
– do –	30/5/18			
– do –	31/5/18			
– " –	– " –	6 P.M.	Route march carried out.	

S. R...
.............LIEUT. COLONEL
COMMG. 17TH (SERVICE) BATT: THE LIVERPOOL REGT.

CONFIDENTIAL.

WAR DIARY.

OF

17th BATTALION "THE KING'S" (LIVERPOOL REGIMENT).

FOR THE MONTH OF JUNE 1918.

VOLUME XXXII.

WAR DIARY
or
INTELLIGENCE SUMMARY.
(Erase heading not required.)

Instructions regarding War Diaries and Intelligence Summaries are contained in F.S. Regs., Part II. and the Staff Manual respectively. Title pages will be prepared in manuscript.

Place	Date	Hour	Summary of Events and Information	Remarks and references to Appendices
INCHEVILLE	1/6/18		Training of 3rd Battalion. 138th Infantry Regiment (U.S. Army) continued.	
do	2/6/18			
do	3/6/18			
do	4/6/18			
do	5/6/18		3rd Bn. 138th Infantry Regt. left INCHEVILLE.	
do	6/6/18		Training Staff engaged in construction of Bombing Pits, Bayonet Fighting Courses, 30 yds. Range, &c. on new Training Ground.	
do	7/6/18			
do	8/6/18		1st Battn. 138th Infantry Regt. arrived.	
do	9/6/18	3 PM	Programme of Training drawn up and discussed with American Unit Commander. Training Staff established liaison with American Unit.	
do	10/6/18		Composite number in Training commenced.	
do	11/6/18		Training continued in following subjects:- Musketry, Bayonet Fighting, Bombing, Lewis Gun, Gas, Field Fortifications, Physical Training, Tactical Exercises, Route Marches. Lectures were given daily by Officers and N.C.O. Instructors. Divine Services.	
do	12/6/18			
do	13/6/18			
do	14/6/18			
do	15/6/18			
do	16/6/18		Training continued on similar lines as previous week.	
do	17/6/18			
do	18/6/18		One Company carried out firing practice on 600 yards Range.	
do	19/6/18			
do	20/6/18	8.15 AM	Training Staff marched with American Units to VISMES-AU-VAL.	See APPENDIX I.
VISMES-AU-VAL	21/6/18	2 PM	Arrived in Billets.	

Army Form C. 2118.

WAR DIARY
or
INTELLIGENCE SUMMARY.
(Erase heading not required.)

Instructions regarding War Diaries and Intelligence Summaries are contained in F.S. Regs., Part II. and the Staff Manual respectively. Title pages will be prepared in manuscript.

Place	Date	Hour	Summary of Events and Information	Remarks and references to Appendices
VISMES-AU-VAL	22/6/18	8 A.M.	Training Staff marched with American Unit to PILLY-LE-HAUT-CLOCHER.	See Appendix II
PILLY-LE-HAUT-CLOCHER	23/6/18	5 P.M.	Arrived in Billets.	
— do —	24/6/18		No Training carried out.	
— do —	25/6/18		Training continued on basis of previous programmes.	
— do —	26/6/18		Owing to Rifle Range now being available no firing was carried out on large range. Targets were fixed, however, in front of a suitable bank and the whole Battalion, including Lewis Guns, practised firing at about 50 yards Range.	
— do —	27/6/18			
— do —	28/6/18	4 P.M.	Training Cadre marched to ST. RIQUIER STATION under orders to proceed to England.	
ST. RIQUIER	— " —	4 P.M.	Entrained.	
ABBEVILLE	— " —	5 P.M.	Detrained and spent night in the Station Rest Camp.	
— do —	29/6/18	9.30 A.M.	Entrained for BOULOGNE.	
BOULOGNE	— " —	4 P.M.	Detrained and proceeded by Motor Lorry to ST. MARTIN'S CAMP.	
— do —	30/6/18	9 A.M.	Left Rest Camp, and embarked at 11.0 am Sailed at 12.30 P.M.	
FOLKESTONE	— " —	3.15 P.M.	Disembarked and entrained immediately for ALDERSHOT.	
ALDERSHOT	— " —	8.10 P.M.	Detrained at NORTH CAMP STATION and marched to MYTCHETT CAMP.	
MYTCHETT CAMP	— " —	8.45 P.M.	Arrived in camp. Battalion transferred to 75th Infantry Bde. 25th Division	

[signature] CAPTAIN.
COMDG: 1/7TH BN "THE KING'S" (LIVERPOOL REGT.).

I

COPY NO. 2

SECRET.
MOVEMENT ORDER BY LIEUT.COL. J.P. PITTS. M.C.
COMDG: 17TH BN. "THE KING'S" (LIVERPOOL REGT).

Thursday, 20th June 1918.

Ref.Map: ABBEVILLE, Sheet.14. 1/100,000.

1. **MOVE.** The 17th Bn. K.L.R. Training Cadre will move to VISMES-AU-VAL Area tomorrow, 21st June 1918.

2. **PARADE.** The Training Staff will parade outside Billets at 8.15 am. ready to move off. Dress - Fighting Order, with Steel Helmets carried on the haversack.

3. **OFFICERS' KITS, BLANKETS, etc.** Blankets and Packs will be dumped at the Quartermaster's Stores at 7.0 am. and G.S. Wagon will then call at the Officers' Mess for Kits, etc.

4. **BILLETS.** Special attention will be paid to cleanliness of billets.

5. **DINNERS.** Dinners will be served on arrival.

6. **ACKNOWLEDGE.**

(sd). W.B. HOLME. Capt. & Adjutant.
17th Battn. K.L.R.

Issued to all concerned by runner at 8/15 p.m., 20.6.18.

Secret.   II   Copy No. 2.

Movement Order by Lt Col. J.P. Pitts M.C.
Comdg: 17th Bn. The King's (Liverpool Regt).

Friday. 21st June 1918.

1. MOVE. The 17th Bn. K.L.R. will move with the attached American Unit to AILLY-LE-HAUT-CLOCHER. Comm. of 22nd inst.

2. PARADE. Training Staff will parade at 7.30 am ready to move off.

3. BLANKETS etc. Blankets and Packs will be dumped in G.S. Wagon at 6.20 am.

4. MEALS. Breakfast - 6.45 am. Haversack Rations will be carried and lunch will be eaten en route.

(Sd). W. B. HOLME.
Capt. + Adjutant
17th K.L.R.

III.

COPY NO. 5.

MOVEMENT ORDER BY LIEUT.COL. J.P. PITTS. M.C.
COMDG: 17TH BN. "THE KING'S" (LIVERPOOL REGT).

Thursday, 27th June 1918.

Reference Map :- ABBEVILLE, 1/100,000.

1. MOVE: The 17th Battn. K.L.R. (less Transport), will entrain at ST. RIQUIER for ENGLAND tomorrow, 28th instant.

2. DETACHMENT. The Detachment at MONFLIERS will move under orders of Capt. E.A. DICKSON. M.C. to entraining station - ST. RIQUIER - and will report at that place at 9.45 am., complete.
   One Blanket per man will be carried, and the remainder of Ordnance Stores will be handed over, if possible, to a British Unit; failing this to an American Unit.
   O.C. Detachment will arrange for the necessary transport from the American Unit to which he is affiliated to convey Officers' Kits, etc. to the station.

3. REMAINDER OF BATTN. Battalion H.Q. and Training Staff at AILLY-LE-HAUT-CLOCHER will parade at 8 am. ready to move off. Dress - Full Marching Order. One Blanket per man will be carried.
   Officers' Kits, Mess Baskets, etc. will be loaded on transport by 7.45 am. and will move off in rear of Unit.
   SQMS. TAYLOR will arrange to collect Officers' Kits at 7.30 am. and supervise loading of Mess Cart.

4. RATIONS. Rations will be drawn for entraining party from the R.S.O., ST. RIQUIER.

5. ACKNOWLEDGE.

(sd). W.B. HOLME. Captain and Adjutant.
17th Battalion K.L.R.

17th King's Liverpool Regt.
----

1. The 17th Bn King's L'pool Regt. (less Transport) will entrain for ENGLAND tomorrow 28th inst.

2. Entraining station - ST.RIQUIER.
   Move to ST.RIQUIER to be complete by 10 a.m.
   Time of train to be notified later.

3. Transport and Transport personnel, 17th King's L'pool Regt. will remain in present location until further orders.

4. Rations can be drawn for entraining party from R.S.O. ST.RIQUIER.

5. No additional transport will be provided.

6. ACKNOWLEDGE.

27.6.18.

Captain,
Brigade Major,
199th Infantry Brigade.

Army Form C 2121
(in pads of 100).

MESSAGES AND SIGNALS.   No of Message............

Code...........	Words.	Charge.	This message is on a/c of:	Rec'd. at........ m
Office of Origin and Service Instructions.	Sent			Date..........
	At..........m.		............Service	From..........
	To..........		(Signature of "Franking Officer.")	By..........
	By..........			

TO ~~7th Bn~~ ~~Hayfield Rfs~~
   ~~A. Frame~~   ~~17 K.R.R.~~
   ~~6 Somer....~~

| Sender's Number. | Day of Month. | In reply to Number. | AAA |
| 0900 | 28 | | |

Confirming this Office 6436/G of 27th. Last time of entrainment at ST RIQUIER 4.30pm. New time of entrainment Pont REMY will be notified later probably in afternoon.

Rec'd 9.20am
28/6/18
Ears

R.D. Otter Major
D.A.Q.M.G.
66 Div

From		
Place		
Time		

The above may be forwarded as now corrected. (Z)

.... Censor. Signature of Addressee or person authorised to telegraph in his name.
*This line should be erased if not required.

www.ingramcontent.com/pod-product-compliance
Lightning Source LLC
Chambersburg PA
CBHW081356160426
43192CB00013B/2419